Silenced Stages

The Loss of Academic Freedom and Campus Policy Debates

SILENCED STAGES

The Loss of Academic Freedom
and Campus Policy Debates

George R. La Noue

RESEARCH PROFESSOR OF POLITICAL SCIENCE
RESEARCH PROFESSOR OF PUBLIC POLICY
SCHOOL OF PUBLIC POLICY
UNIVERSITY OF MARYLAND, BALTIMORE COUNTY

CAROLINA ACADEMIC PRESS
Durham, North Carolina

See catalog.loc.gov for Library of Congress Cataloging-in-Publication Data

ISBN 978-1-5310-1602-9
e-ISBN 978-1-5310-1603-6

Cover design Revere La Noue, rl@reverelanoue.com
falconbridge.collection.com

The research grant on which this book is based was administered by the Maryland In-stitute of Policy Analysis and Research. This book is a major extension and updating of papers given at the Policy History Association, the American Political Science Associa-tion, and the American Legislative Exchange Council conferences in 2016 and articles published in *Academic Questions* and by The Heterodox Academy and the James G. Martin Center.

While the opinions expressed are those of the lead author alone, he is greatly in-debted to the project's student research team (Kamilla Keldiyarova, UMBC School of Public Policy, MPP student (liberal arts colleges); David Song, Stanford University School of Education, Ph.D. student (top private and public universities); Dan Smyth, UMBC School of Public Policy MPP graduate (liberal arts colleges); Matthew Speake, University of Baltimore Law School, J.D. student (regional public and private univer-sities); and Adam Shulman, UMBC School of Public Policy, Ph.D. student (religious universities).

Carolina Academic Press
700 Kent Street
Durham, North Carolina 27701
Telephone (919) 489-7486
Fax (919) 493-5668
www.cap-press.com

Printed in the United States of America

Contents

Synopsis

Recently, many American higher education institutions have endured politically motivated disturbances undermining academic freedom. Unlike the wave of disruptions under the expanded "free speech" banner in the Sixties, these new protests have often sought to limit the speech of invited speakers, campus spokespersons, and the media with whom they disagreed. In response, many prominent persons, including former President Obama, university leaders, and faculty senates have sought to restore the primacy of open dialogue as an academic ideal.

The barking dog of censorship usually creates attention. This book discusses incidents that created national publicity at Amherst, Brown, City University of New York, Evergreen, Lewis and Clark, Michigan, Middlebury, New York University, Reed, Seattle, Yale, UC Berkeley, University of Pennsylvania, University of Washington, Vanderbilt, Wesleyan, and Williams. But, if that guard dog just silently patrols the fences of acceptable campus discourse, nothing may be heard in the vacuum created. Many speakers will not be invited and many public policy issues will be thought too controversial for open discussion. Even tenured faculty may avoid expressing ideas that will upset their colleagues or campus activists. **For free speech, the problem may be more often what is omitted from campus discussions, the silenced stages, than overt suppression.**

This book reports on original research about the topics and participants in on-campus policy debates or forums where divergent viewpoints were presented regarding 24 national policy areas. Accessing campus calendars for 2014 and 2015 in a stratified national sample of 97 universities and colleges and 28 law schools enrolling 991,802 students annually, the results show a paucity of such events, except at very elite wealthy institutions or law schools. For most students in American higher education, the opportunity to hear on-campus debates about important public policy issues does not exist. Free speech for controversial speakers dominates the press coverage, but the more important story of the absence of debate and divergent opinion is missed.

Since almost all higher education institutions affirm as part of their mission the training of engaged citizens and almost all students can vote, what accounts for such limited planned policy discourse on campus? This book suggests several theories. (1) Academic management has become more corporate and seeks to avoid controversy. (2) Despite the proliferation of campus administrators, no one is responsible for seeing that a well-balanced political discourse exists. (3) Campus cultures vigorously promote attractive student living, recreational activities, and career preparation with little organized focus on informed citizenship. Their ethos also emphasizes tolerance and inclusion for all, while fearing disturbing ideas that might arguably create a hostile learning environment for any group. (4) Faculty reward structures do not incentivize them to organize or participate in policy debates. (5) Professors, in fields most concerned with policy issues, are increasingly politically and ideologically homogeneous and may not see the need for their views to be debated.

After reviewing relevant judicial decisions on free speech, the role of debate in the formation of our political institutions, and some useful campus experiments in intellectual diversity, this book turns to the question of what can be done about the failure to promote actively these values across higher education.

The solutions must be scalable, inexpensive, and most of all compatible with the announced values of the academy. First, trustees and legislatures should ask the institutions accountable to them for annual reports describing what campuses have done to expose all their students to diverse opinions about the great policy issues relevant to casting an informed vote. Second, institutions should designate some administrative office or faculty committee to plan and evaluate whether scheduled campus-wide events fulfill the mission of diverse civic education for all students. Third, institutions should be certain their campus activities calendars are accessible and maintained, so that programming efforts and balanced intellectual diversity can be observed by everyone in the community. If a campus does not have the resources to provide balanced programming, research centers, think tanks etc.

should provide up-to-date materials on the Internet for local use. Fourth, funders should ask the question of whether campuses are fulfilling their announced civic missions in considering support. Fifth, students and parents in evaluating the intellectual climate of a campus should ask for information assuring them that diverse viewpoints on public policy issues are expressed and respected.

The withdrawal of campuses from a culture of vigorous political debate does not auger well for the future of American democracy, where dependence on rational and civil consideration of complex policy alternatives is essential.

About the Author

George La Noue is Research Professor of Political Science and Research Professor of Public Policy at the University of Maryland Baltimore County. He served as Director of Policy Sciences, one of the largest programs in the graduate school enrolling about 180 Masters and Ph.D. students, for eighteen years. Prior to coming to the University of Maryland, he was Director of the Teacher's College-Columbia University Graduate Program in Politics and Education. He has taught at American University, the University of Chicago, the University of Miami, and the University of Strasbourg (France).

He graduated *magna cum laude* from Hanover College in 1959 and received his M.A. in 1961 and Ph.D. in 1966 in Political Science from Yale University. He has been awarded three national fellowships (the Woodrow Wilson, Danforth, and Public Administration) and two international fellowships in Sweden and Germany.

Dr. La Noue's research has focused on education policy, civil rights law and public program analysis. He has published five books and numerous articles. His book, *Academics in Court: the Consequences of Academic Discrimination Litigation*, University of Michigan Press, was funded by the Carnegie Corporation of New York. His book, *The Politics of School Decentralization* was published by D.C. Heath. Earlier he edited a book, *Educational Vouchers: Concepts and Controversies*, for Teachers College Press. His most recent book, *Improbable Excellence: The Saga of UMBC,* was published in 2016 in connection with that University's 50th anniversary. He is the author of four encyclopedia entries: "School Decentralization," *Encyclopedia of Education,* "Political Science," *Encyclopedia of Educational Research*, and "Affirmative

Action," *World Book Encyclopedia* and in the *Encyclopedia of Political Science*. He is the author of eleven law review articles.

Professor La Noue has served as President of the Politics of Education Society, as a member of the Editorial Board of *Education and Urban Society*, as a member of the Maryland State Commission on Public School Athletics, the Maryland Department of Education's Commission on Charter Schools, the Maryland State Commission on Equal Pay, the Faculty Advisory Committee of the Maryland State Board for Higher Education, the Truancy Reduction Project of the Administrative Office of the [Maryland] Courts, and chaired the Task Force on Higher Education of the United States Equal Employment Opportunity Commission. He was appointed by Baltimore Mayor Kurt Schmoke to serve as a member of the Mayor's Task Force on School Choice. He was also the academic member of the National Institute for Government Purchaser's Universal Certification Committee which certifies procurement officers in the United States, Canada, and Ireland. He has been Vice-Chairman of the Maryland Civil Rights Advisory Committee.

A frequent witness in Congressional testimony, Dr. La Noue is also a well-seasoned trial expert on civil rights cases in federal courts. He has been an Assistant to the Executive Director of the U.S. Equal Employment Opportunity Commission and has been the U.S. Department of Labor's principal trial expert in academic equal pay litigation. He has also served as consultant on a wide variety of educational and legal problems to the American Civil Liberties Union, the American Alliance for Rights and Responsibilities, the Association of Governing Boards, the National Council of Churches, the U.S. Department of Education Office of Civil Rights, the U. S. Commission on Civil Rights, and several state governments and universities.

Sponsored by the U.S. Information Agency, the Swedish government, the German government, the Fredrich Ebert Foundation, and others, Dr. La Noue has had the opportunity to do research and lecture in sixteen countries.

Silenced Stages

The Loss of Academic Freedom
and Campus Policy Debates

Chapter I
Introduction

In American higher education both public and private institutions affirm the mission of producing enlightened citizens and leaders.[1] It is an old tradition, harkening back to the founder of the University of Virginia, Thomas Jefferson, who once declared "If a nation expects to be ignorant and free, in a state of civilization, it expects what never was and never will be."[2]

After the 2016 national election, Frederick M. Lawrence, Chief Executive Officer of Phi Beta Kappa, wrote:

> Now, with our country so deeply divided, it is more important than ever for us to be seekers of truth . . . perhaps especially in dialogue with those with whom we have fundamental disagreements. Nothing can transform someone into an effective seeker of the truth better than a liberal arts and sciences education.

---

1. American Association of Colleges and Universities, *A Crucible Moment: College Learning and Democracy's Future* (2012). American Council of Trustees and Alumni, "No U.S. History?" July 2016, p.7. Other organizations also have found huge deficits in the information among Americans about their government and history. If 40% of college graduates didn't know that the power to declare war belongs to Congress and a third of adult Americans can't identify the three branches of our government, then the chances are not encouraging that they are familiar with the policy options for even our most pressing political problems. Anthony Henning, "Colleges Reject the Duty to Teach Liberty's Framework," The James G. Martin Center, July 4, 2018.

2. Thomas Jefferson letter to Colonel Paul L Ford, January 6, 1816. Paul L. Ford, ed. *The Writings of Thomas Jefferson* (New York: Cosimo Classics, 2010) Vol. 10, p. 4.

Lawrence went on to discuss Supreme Court Justice Louis D. Brandeis' concept of the role of the private citizen "which cannot be neglected under a republican form of government without serious injury to the public." Brandeis argued there were three functions of the private citizen: first, to turn raw information into knowledge; second, to evaluate arguments; and, finally, to engage in reasoned debates. "Once," he said, "we are able to determine the validity of another's point of view, we can present our own understanding of events and circumstances in a logical and comprehensive manner."[3]

At least abstractly, academic and political leaders concur that in order to achieve civic enlightenment, students should be exposed to and hear debated a variety of policy viewpoints. But something has gone wrong with this bedrock principle in the nation's colleges and universities.

In 2015, President Obama criticized the use of political tests circumscribing campus speech and advocated that students be exposed to different viewpoints:

> Look, the purpose of college is not just, as I said before, to transmit skills. It is also to widen your horizons; to make you a better citizen, to help evaluate information, to help you make your way in the world; to help you be more creative. The way to do that is to create a space where a lot of ideas are presented and collide and people having arguments and people are testing each other's theories, and over time people learn from each other because they are getting out of their own narrow point of view and having a broader point of view.[4]

Much has been written about the anti-free speech policies and practices that characterize many of our nation's campuses and of the ideological uniformity that infects many of their academic departments.[5] What has

---

3. Frederick M. Lawrence, "Rediscovering the role of public citizen and the art of public discourse." *The Hill*, November 14, 2016.

4. Transcript of a town hall meeting in Des Moines Iowa, September 14, 2015.

5. Paul Berman, editor, *Debating P.C. The Controversy over Political Correctness on College Campuses* (New York: Dell Publishing,1992); Mary Katherine Ham and Guy Benson, *End of Discussion, How the Left's Outrage Industry Shuts Down Debate* (New York: Crown Forum 2015); Charles J. Sykes, *Fail U. The False Promise of Higher Education* (New York: St. Martin's Press, 2016), *Chapter 11;* Timothy Garton Ash, *Free Speech: Ten Principles for a Connected World* (New Haven: Yale University Press, 2016); Ben-Porath, Sigal, *Free Speech on*

not been examined empirically are the topics and participants in actual on-campus public policy debates. What are the subjects of reasoned discourse is as important as what is disrupted. This research will explore that subject and some of the reasons for the narrowing of the scope of acceptable speech in higher education.

The intemperate character of recent political discourse threatens the intelligent appraisal of policy alternatives on which democracy depends. The tendency in higher education to restrict speech and ignore policy debates also should be worrisome to the general public. Almost all students are eligible to vote. Where during students' educations will they be exposed to divergent viewpoints and serious substantive information about important policy questions affecting their personal prospects and the nation's future? Where will they learn that reasonable people can disagree civilly about these issues and that good citizenship requires a tolerant respectful hearing of ideas that initially may seem disagreeable?

In the name of enforced harmony, recently, there have been disturbing instances when commencement and other speakers have been successfully disinvited or threatened with disruption after some students objected to the viewpoint they thought would be expressed (Christine Lagarde—Smith, Ayaan Hirsi Ali—Brandeis, Condoleezza Rice—Rutgers and Smith, Henry Kissinger—New York University, Robert Birgeneau—Haverford, Robert Zoellick—Swarthmore, and Bill Maher—UC Berkeley). At other campuses, particularly those with strong religious identities, speakers have been disinvited by administrations when the invitees' religious orthodoxy was questioned.[6]

Campus (Philadelphia: University of Pennsylvania Press, 2017); Wendy Kaminer, "The progressive ideas behind the lack of free speech on campus," *The Washington Post*, February 20, 2015; Kathleen Parker, "Trigger Warnings, Colleges and the 'Swaddled Generation,'" *The Washington Post*, May 19, 2015, Eugene Volokh, "American University faculty resolution on freedom of expression (and in particular trigger warnings)," *The Washington Post*, September 22, 2015, George F. Will, "A summer break from campus muzzling," *The Washington Post*, May 29, 2015 and Robert P. George, "Why Academic Freedom Matters (Now More Than Ever)," Intercollegiate Review Online, June 18, 2018.

6. Libby Nelson, "British Theologian uninvited from the University of San Diego," *Inside Higher Education,* November 2, 2012. On the other hand, the University of Notre Dame decided to go ahead with honoring President Barack Obama, Vice-President Joe Biden, and Speaker John Boehner (the latter two prominent Catholic laymen) despite strong outside opposition to some of the invitees' political positions which conflicted with church doctrine. Some Notre Dame administrators objected to inviting President Trump to campus

After Michael Bloomberg, former New York Mayor and philanthropist, was invited to give the 2014 Harvard University commencement address, protesters criticized his selection because he had supported "stop and frisk" policing that impacted more heavily on black and Latino New Yorkers. They argued that extending "an invitation to someone who alienates entire segments of the student body is ill-advised and worthy of condemnation."[7]

Bloomberg decided to speak anyway declaring:

> Tolerance for other people's ideas and the freedom to express your own are inseparable values at great universities. . . . Joined together, they form a sacred trust that holds the basis of our democratic society. But that trust is perpetually vulnerable to the tyrannical tendencies of monarchs, mobs, and majorities. And lately, we've seen those tendencies manifest themselves too often both on college campuses and in our society.[8]

Suppressing speech of those "with incorrect" ideas is not, of course, a new phenomenon. During the McCarthy era, professors, journalists, and artists were harassed, if they expressed doubts about American foreign or domestic policies by zealots on the right.[9] As Alan Bloom has pointed out, however:

---

because of his immigration policies, so Vice President and former Indiana Governor, Mike Pence was invited in his stead. After some Gonzaga University alumni organized a petition against Bishop Desmond Tutu's invitation to be the 2012 commencement speaker. The student newspaper ran a forum pro and con and one student wrote: "It is especially the beauty of a Jesuit university such as this, encouraging healthy and intelligent discussions, not discrediting someone because we disagree. Last time I checked, disagreeing with Church doctrine didn't mean you couldn't participate. Unless, of course, the Inquisition, is still flourishing." Scott Jaschik, *"Protest Over Bishop Tutu as Speaker at Gonzaga," Inside Higher Education,* April 12, 2012.

7. Scott Jaschik, "Harvard Debates Bloomberg as Commencement Speaker," *Inside Higher Education,* March 14, 2014.

8. As quoted in Kristen Powers, *The Silencing: How the Left is Killing Free Speech* (Washington, D.C: Regnery Publishing, 2015), pp. 92–93. See also Matt Richelieu, "Bloomberg assails lack of tolerance for diverse ideas," *Boston Globe,* May 29, 2014.

9. The classic works on the development of academic freedom are Richard Hofstadter, *Academic Freedom in the Age of the College* (Piscataway, N.J.: Transaction Press, reprinted 1995) and Walter P. Metzger, *Academic Freedom in the Age of the University* (New York: Columbia University Press, 1961). For a more recent overview of academic freedom with multiple perspectives, see the seventeen essays in Akeel Bilgrami (eds.) and Jonathan R. Cole

… the McCarthy period was the last time the university had a sense of community, defined as a common enemy McCarthy, those like him, and those that followed them, were clearly nonacademic and antiacademic, the barbarians at the gates. In major universities they had no effect whatsoever on curriculum or appointments. The range of thought and speech that took place within them was unaffected. Academic freedom had for that last moment more than an abstract meaning, a content with respect to research and publication about which there was general agreement.[10]

This era proved fleeting. In his history of academic freedom, Donald Alexander Downs, Professor of Political Science, Law and Journalism at University of Wisconsin Madison, concluded:

During most of the twentieth century, threats to campus free speech and academic freedom came mostly from the right and from *outside* institutions of higher learning. The new attacks on free thought that arose in the latter 1980s turned this pattern on its head: they have arisen from leftist sources *inside* the ivory tower. It is for this reason that new battles over free speech have sometimes taken on the characteristics of civil wars. The new type of censorship is "progressive" in aspirations, not "reactionary.". . . progressive censorship has a way of producing illiberal, repressive consequences that are just as detrimental to open universities and minds as traditional forms of censorship.[11]

Former Vice President Joe Biden, speaking at a joint University of Delaware event, with Republican Governor John Kasich, recalled:

(eds.), *Who's Afraid of Academic Freedom* (New York: Columbia University Press, 2015). Also Joanna Williams, *Academic Freedom in an Age of Conformity* (Basingstoke, U.K.: Palgrave McMillan 2016).

10. Alan Bloom, *Closing of the American Mind* (New York: Simon and Schuster, 1987), p. 324.

11. Donald Alexander Downs, *Restoring Free Speech and Liberty on Campuses* (Oakland, Ca.: The Independent Institute 2005) distributed by Cambridge University Press. A case study about the ideological shifts in support of campus censorship can be found in Mike Adams and Adam Kissel, "Censorship in the UNC System: Correcting the Narrative," *Academic Questions,* Summer 2017, Vol. 30, No.2. pp. 210–223. See also, Philip Lee, *Academic Freedom and American Universities* (Lanham, MD.: Lexington Books, 2016).

When I was coming up through College and graduate school free speech was a big issue. But it was the opposite. It was liberals who were shouted down when they spoke. Liberals have very short memories. I mean it sincerely. We [liberals] hurt ourselves badly when we don't allow speech to take place. If your idea is big enough, it should be able to compete. And you should be able to listen to another point of view, as virulent as it may be, and reject it, expose it. . . . The First Amendment is one of the defining features of who we are in the Bill of Rights, and to shut it down in the name of what is appropriate is wrong. Simply wrong.[12]

Accepting those perspectives, this research focuses on speech within the academy. When some anonymous troll uses the Internet to demean some outspoken faculty member or some legislator playing to his constituents' anxieties threatens academic freedom, those actions should be criticized. When those on campus suppress speech, however, then the responsibility of those who work or live there to protect academic freedom is greater.

According to the Foundation for Individual Rights in Education (F.I.R.E.), the trend of trying to disinvite speakers is increasing. Their research shows in the twenty-two year period between 1987 and 2008, 138 protests of scheduled speeches resulted in 62 publicized incidents where the invited guest did not speak. More recently, it took only six years (2009 to 2014) to have another 62 speeches canceled. The aborted speeches affect both liberal and conservative speakers, though the latter were affected twice as often.[13] Student attempts to deny invited speakers the right to be heard is not just a United States' practice. "No platforming" as it is often called has occurred in Australia,[14] Canada[15] and the United Kingdom.[16]

---

12. Nikita Vladimirov, "Biden: Liberals 'hurt ourselves badly by opposing free speech,'" *Campus Reform*, October 19, 2017.

13. Powers, p.7.

14. Caroline Mel, "Threat to Free Speech Spreads to Australian Campuses," http://heterodoxacademy.org/2017/09/ threat-to-free-spreads.

15. Scott Jaschik, "U British Columbia Restores Invitation to Speaker," *Inside Higher Education*, January 10, 2016. For a discussion of the controversy at a Canadian university over showing a recorded television debate in a communications class on the use of gender pronouns see Raffi Grinberg, "Lindsey Shepard and the Potential for Heterodoxy at Wilfrid Laurier University." *The Heterodox Academy* website, November, 23, 2017.

16. The National Union of Students of the United Kingdom No Platform Policy states no "individual or members of organizations identified by the Democratic Procedures

Equally important, how many prospective speakers were never even considered for invitations because of the threat of campus protests? How many subjects are not debated on campus because some might be disturbed by hearing viewpoints with which they do not agree?

A. Campus Controversies

Before reporting results of the research on the actual topics and participants in American on-campus debates in 2014 and 2015, describing some recent well-publicized freedom of speech controversies provides a context. Often student demands were not to increase dialogue or debate, but to restrict it and to punish those with whom they disagreed.[17] Some argued that it would be acceptable to have a speech on campus, so long as the speaker was not awarded an honorary degree, but that distinction has not always been observed. Objections to permitting a speaker on campus have been successful, even if funded by an outside group using an ordinary lecture format.

At California's Scripps College, the women's campus of the Claremont Colleges Consortium, the Elizabeth Hubert Malott Public Affairs Program,

Committee as holding racist or fascist views" may attend or speak at any NUS function or conference nor can any NUS official share a platform with any racist or fascist. NUS has identified several Muslim and right wing groups that fit its definition. The policy has created controversies at Oxford and Cambridge where protests were lodged against speeches by government ministers. At the University of Durham a debate on multiculturalism was threatened with disruption and then cancelled. http://wikipedia.org/wiki/NUS_No_Platform_Policy. A survey of UK universities by the online magazine Spiked, found 94% had some restrictions on free speech. Two issues were must subject to censorship: discussions of religion and transgenderism. http://w.w.w.universityobserver.i.e.news/94-of-uk-univeri-ties-restrict-freedom-of-speech. In 2015, students at Cardiff University (Wales) petitioned to prevent feminist Germaine Greer from speaking on the grounds that her views on transgendered women were transphobic and misogynist. Greer went ahead with her talk on "Women & Power: The Lessons of the 20th Century." In January, 2018, Jo Johnson, the UK minister for higher education announced a plan to create new government office that would have the authority to fine universities that do not uphold freedom of speech. She declared: "However, well intentioned, the proliferation of such safe spaces, the rise of no platforming, the removal of 'offensive' books from libraries, and the drawing up of ever more extensive lists of banned 'trigger' words are undermining the principle of free speech in our universities." Scott Jaschik, "Britain May Fine Universities That Limit Free Speech," *Inside Higher Education*, January 2, 2018.

17. For a list of various demands in the 2015 student protests see TheDemands.org representing some 72 different campuses.

in memory of that former alumni and trustee, was established by her family. The purpose of these lectures was to manifest "her belief that a range of opinions about the world—especially opinions with which we may disagree, or think we do not agree— leads to a better educational experience." The primary audience was Scripps College students, but the lectures were open to the other Consortium Colleges and the general public.

Examining the list of Malott series speakers from 2006 to 2015, it is evident that they were drawn from the pool of nationally known personalities from the political right spectrum. Perhaps one reason for these endowed lectures is the lack of partisan diversity in the Colleges. Claremont McKenna Professor Emeritus Ward Elliot has examined this issue in annual surveys. In his most recent report, he found no Scripps faculty were registered Republicans and, of the 532 Claremont Colleges core faculty, only 15 were Republicans.[18]

In the spring of 2015, Barbara Pierce Bush, co-founder and CEO of the Global Health Corps which is dedicated "to improving access to healthcare in some of the world's most underserved areas," was the speaker.[19] For the fall of 2015, the lecture series invited to Scripps, George Will, nationally syndicated Pulitzer Prize winning columnist and author of fourteen books. Earlier on June 6, he had written a column criticizing the federal Office of Civil Rights (OCR) new Title IX requirement that campuses use the "preponderance of evidence" standard "rather than the "clear and convincing proof" test courts use in adjudicating allegations of rape or other sexual assaults. Will thought that lower standard of proof requirement privileged sex-related charges over claims about other crimes. A number of Harvard and Penn Law faculty agreed in general with his position.[20]

In his usual acerbic style, Will wrote a truncated op-ed column that read:

18. Brad Richardson, "George Will, Uninvited From Scripps College, *The Claremont Independent,* October 6, 2015. For a subsequent controversy over a Scripps College invitation see Rosanna Xiu, "Scripps College nabbed Madeline Albright as its commencement speaker—and then the war broke out," *Los Angeles Times,* May 9, 2016.

19. Elizabeth Hubert Malott Public Affairs Program events, http://www.scrippscollege.edu/events (accessed 9/29/2015).

20. "Rethink Harvard's Sexual Harassment Policy," (letter signed by 28 member of the Harvard Law Faculty) *Boston Globe,* October 15, 2015. Open Letter from [16] Members of the Penn Law Faculty, *Wall Street Journal* Online, October 17, 2014.

[Colleges and universities] are learning that when they say campus victimizations are ubiquitous (micro-aggressions; often not discernable to the untutored eye, are everywhere), and when they make victimhood a coveted status that confers privileged status, victims proliferate. And academia's progressivism has rendered it intellectually defenseless now that progressivism's achievement, the regulatory state, has decided it is academia's turn to be broken to government's saddle.[21]

The column was widely criticized and his Scripps lecture was cancelled. That set off 118 posts on the disinvitation on a Scripps blog called Pingback. Some of the comments engaged the philosophical issues involved: "It's [Will's] prerogative to write that. It's also Scripps' prerogative to use the column as an indication that he isn't someone they want representing intellectual diversity on their campus."[22] Another comment, hopefully not written by a college student, proclaimed "George Will is a sick man. He was rightly rewarded by God with a Downs Syndrome kid."[23] The idea that Will should appear on campus and that his views be vigorously debated did seem to the commentators to be the obvious solution. The national debate over Title IX rules for adjudicating claims of sexual assault continues vigorously, but on most campuses the issue is confined to administrative edicts with little face-to-face public dialogue with those of different perspectives.[24]

On the other side of the continent, Williams College, with an endowment of over $2.5 billion and often considered the top liberal arts college in the country, also faced student push-back over a speaker invitation. Its student-led, alumni-funded lecture series called "Uncomfortable Learning" has the purpose "to expose students to controversial voices and opinions they might otherwise hear." When the series invited writer Suzanne Venker to speak, her lecture title was to be "One Step Forward, Ten Steps Back:

---

21. George Will, "Colleges become the victim of progressivism," *The Washington Post*, June 6, 2014.

22. Richardson, *The Claremont Independent*, Pingback blog.

23. Ibid.

24. For a useful recent history of the Title IX adjudication issues, see the three part series by Emily Yoffe. "The Uncomfortable Truth About Campus Rape Policy," *The Atlantic*, September 6, 2017.

Why Feminism Fails."[25] The provocative title began to attract "acerbic comments" on the forum's face book page. That began to worry Zach Wood, an African-American and forum leader. One Facebook commentator wrote:

> When you bring a misogynistic, white supremacist men's right's activist to campus in the name of 'dialogue' and 'the other side,' you are not only causing actual mental, social, psychological and physical harm to students, but you are also—paying—for the continued dispersal of violent ideologies that that kill and harm black and brown (trans) sisters . . . you are dripping your hands in their blood, Zach Wood.[26]

The comment, since erased from the forum's Facebook page might seem like a parody, but Mr. Wood was sufficiently concerned that he canceled Ms. Venker's speech. He said, that even in such a bucolic setting as Williamstown, Massachusetts, "people would get riled up while she was speaking, maybe even throw things and there wasn't enough time before the event to organize security. You never know. We're just trying to think ahead. The last thing we wanted to do was something destructive."[27]

Wood was philosophical about capitulating to the Heckler's Veto. He said, "If it was just my decision, I would have brought Venker to campus. . . . Suzanne's Venker's views are held by millions of Americans whether we like it or not, and if we want to push back, we have to try to understand them."[28]

An editorial in the Williams college paper disagreed:

> In general, the College should not allow speech that challenges fundamental human rights and devalues people based on identity markers, like being a woman. Much of what Venker has said online, in her books and in interviews fall in this category. While free speech is important and there are problems with deeming speech unacceptable, students must not be unduly exposed to harmful stereotypes in order to live and learn here without suffering emotional injury. It is possible that some speech is too harmful to invite to campus. The College

---

25. Josh Logue, "Williams student revoke invitation to speaker who criticizes feminism," *Inside Higher Education*, October 21, 2015. Two years later, Wood's fears were realized when reactions to Charles Murray's speech at "bucolic" Middlebury College turned violent.

26. Ibid.

27. Ibid.

28. Ibid.

should be a safe space for students where people respect others' identities. Venker's appearance would be an invasion of that space.[29]

Williams College's initial administrative statement on this incident, which became a national controversy, was the cancellation was a student's decision, not an institutional one.

In October 2017, the Uncomfortable Learning Series brought Christine Hoff Sommers, the author of several books, including *The War Against Boys*, to speak. Her lecture went forward but according to Wood, the students who attended made personal attacks, directed either at her or at me for inviting her, calling Sommers "stupid, harmful, a white supremacist."[30] Wood concluded:

> At Williams, the administration promotes social tolerance at the expense of political tolerance. I cannot name a single conservative speaker that has been brought to the campus by the administration. In classrooms, liberal arguments are often treated as unquestionable truths. In some cases, conservative students even feel the need to refrain from stating their opinion for fear of being shut down or strongly disliked for doing so.[31]

Zach Wood, however, literally had the last word. In 2018, he graduated, became a Robert I. Bartley Fellow with the *Wall Street Journal,* and published his autobiography to critical acclaim. After recounting the personal threats he received, Wood recalled in his book:

> I tried explaining to my fellow students that I wasn't doing this [leading Uncomfortable Learning] because I was secretly a conservative, a self-hating black man, or anti-feminist, men's right activist. Rather, I was sick of living in an echo chamber. At Williams, most of my professors taught their perspective on any given issue as if it were fact instead of delving into opposing views to create well-rounded lessons. Around

29. "Anti-Feminist Speaker Disinvited to 'Uncomfortable Learning' Lecture Series. http://reason.com/blog/2015/10/21/vendker-feminist-speaker-williams-college.

30. George Leef, "When a Black Student Dares to Speak up for Free Speech," https://www.jamesgmartin center/2017/12/black-student.

31. Zachary Wood, "At Williams, a Funny Way of "Listening." *Wall Street Journal,* November 17, 2017. Naturally, there is a You Tube of the event.

campus, progressive ideas were lauded, while conservative ones were shut down for being insensitive. The few conservatives at Williams were largely scared into silence, knowing that if they went against the status quo they would often be labeled as biased and wrong.[32]

Even the cornerstone of free speech, a free press, has been affected by the movement toward enforcing conformity. On several campuses, offended students have retaliated against their newspapers by stealing copies, so their classmates would not be infected by objectionable words or ideas. Destroying paper is a strange behavior by the most electronically-connected generation in history. But there are other ways to suppress ideas annoying to some students.

In September 2015, a sophomore and 30 year-old Iraq War veteran wrote an op-ed for the *Argus,* Wesleyan University's (CT) student newspaper.[33] He suggested that the Black Lives Matter movement might influence increased violence against police officers. Those offended did not ask for a right of rebuttal on that issue which they surely would have received. Instead copies of the paper were stolen and 140 students and some faculty signed a petition demanding that the 150 year-old newspaper be partially defunded, that a dedicated column on the paper's front page for "minority voices" be created, and that "diversity training" for all members of campus publications be required.[34] Student government leaders who signed the petition explained that:

> We hope that the cries for change from the students of color community will move the *Argus* leadership to action. . . . This past spring, we initiated a complete constitutional and tonal restructuring of the Wesleyan Student Association to elevate marginalized and historically unrepresented voices that we felt so desperately needed to be heard on campus. . . . The *Argus* can make this change as well.[35]

---

32. Zachery R. Wood, *Uncensored: My Life and Uncomfortable Conversations at the Intersection of Black and White America* (New York: Dutton, 2018) p. 3.

33. Bryan Stascavage, "Why the Black Lives Matter Isn't What You Think," *Wesleyan Argus,* September 14, 2015.

34. Catherine Rampell, "Free speech is flunking out on college campuses," *The Washington Post,* October 22, 2105.

35. Frederick M. Hess, "Lukewarm Column on 'Black lives matter' sparks demand for reeducation," *National Review,* September 23, 2015.

Embarrassed by the national publicity created by this apparent effort to censor or manipulate the newspaper, Michael Roth, Wesleyan's President, as well its provost and its vice president for equity and inclusion, responded:

> Debates can raise intense emotions, but it doesn't mean that we should demand ideological conformity because people are made uncomfortable. As members of a university community, we always have right to respond with our own opinions, but there is no right not to be offended. We certainly have no right to harass people because we don't like their views.[36]

Some Wesleyan student activists were not impressed with the University's freedom of speech position calling it a luxury and a smoke screen. They wrote:

> Freedom of speech, in its popular understanding, does not protect Black Lives Matter advocates who are trying to survive in a racist world, but instead protects the belief systems of dominant people—despite the extent of their heightened ignorance... By focusing on freedom of speech instead of students' lives and ability to safely exist on this campus, you are practicing censorship and partaking in racism.[37]

A few years later, perhaps in response to the embarrassment the newspaper censorship incident caused and stimulated by a $3 million gift from a trustee, Wesleyan began to offer courses and programs on topics such as "the philosophical and economic foundations of private property, free enterprise, and market economies" and "the relationship of tolerance to individual rights, freedom, and voluntary associations."[38]

---

36. Ibid., p. 2.

37. "An Open Letter to the Wesleyan Community from Students of Color." Posted at: wesleying.org/2015/09/25. As quoted by Sykes, *Fail U*, p. 156.

38. Jeremy Willinger, "The Opening of the Liberal Mind," WSJ op-ed by Wesleyan President Michael S. Roth, The Heterodox Academy, May 11, 2017. President Roth reported to the first annual conference of The Heterodox Academy (New York City June 15, 2018) that one of his trustees remarked that the student veteran who had sparked the *Argus* controversy had survived Fallujah and hoped he would survive Wesleyan. President Roth also identified several groups who he thought brought diversity to the campus and began dia-

Other campus protestors have sought to restrict the press, unless its members advocated their view point. At Smith College in November 2015, a bi-racial coalition demonstrated to call attention to racism at Smith and in support of similar protests on other campuses. The demonstrators wanted press coverage, but Alyssa Mata-Flores, a student organizer stated:

> We are asking that any journalist or press that cover our story participate and articulate their solidarity with black students and other students of color. By taking a neutral stance, journalists and the media are being complacent in our fight. . . . Organizers said journalists were welcome to cover the event if they agreed to explicitly state they supported the movement in their articles.[39]

When journalists objected to these rules, Smith administrators responded: "On balance as strongly as the College prefers to err on the side of a campus open to the media, the students' opposition to it at their own event-which they had created and were hosting-was honored." A journalist writing about these events commented, "College should be a time and place for a freewheeling exchange of ideas, for exploration, for putting your views to the test. Not for hunkering down in a safe cocoon." Though Smith would have preferred to "err" on the side of free speech, in the end it deferred to its students/customers.[40]

In the spring of 2018, a debate was to take place on the Lafayette College campus on the topic of nationalism versus globalism. College President Alison Byerly invited Nigel Farage, former leader of the UK Independence Party, prominent advocate of the Brexit movement, and the *London Times* "Briton of the Year for 2014," to represent the nationalism side. This drew

---

logues with them. After conducting several such meetings, he received a request for similar discussions from some conservative Christians, who Roth was surprised to find even existed at Wesleyan. A description of this unusual conference can be found in Andy Ngo, "Can Heterodoxy Save the Academy," *Quillette,* June 22, 2018.

39. Rem Rieder, "Campuses Need a Refresher Course in the First Amendment," *USA Today*, November 24, 2015.

40. College newspapers have a variety of relationships with their host institutions. Some are by long tradition completely independent, financed by advertisements, and/or student fees. Others are financially supported by the institution which exercises some control over the press to avoid libel and conflicts with doctrinal issues, if the school has a religious affiliation Jeremy Bauer-Wolf, "New student coalition alleges press is suppressed at Christian institutions," *Inside Higher Education*, May 23, 2018.

a condemnation from the campus Hillel, the Muslim Students Association, the International Students Association, and the Association of Black Collegians. They contended Farage's viewpoints were contrary to campus non-discrimination policies because "we all deserve to feel at home here." The students continued:

> We fear not only the effects that this event may have on our campus discourse but further the emotional harm and physical harm Farage's comments may initiate. We feel his capacity to inflict emotional harm and his potential to incite violence against campus groups make him not a purveyor of free speech, but a harbinger of an uncomfortable, unsafe residential environment.[41]

The obligation to protect students from emotional injury was addressed by *New York Times* columnist Bret Stephens in a speech at the University of Michigan on February 20, 2018. He said the purpose of free speech is not just to:

> hear our own voices, or the voices of those with whom we already agree, it is also to hear what other people, with other views, often anathema to ours, have to say. To hear such speech may make us uncomfortable. As well it should. Discomfort is not injury. An intellectual provocation is not a physical assault. It's a stimulus. Over time, it can improve our own arguments, and sometimes even change our minds. . . . Democracy is enriched if you do. So are you.[42]

In the fall of 2015, probably the most publicized confrontation over free speech in a private institution occurred at venerable, elite, and wealthy Yale University (full disclosure my graduate school alma mater). The triggering incident was a dispute over whether the college should issue rules about potentially offensive Halloween costumes. Obviously neither a cowboy nor an Indian be, but the episode ended in a large demonstration, intense campus discussions, and a commitment from Yale to meet many of the protes-

---

41. "Lafayette should not welcome harmful speech," *The Lafayette,* https://www.lafayette studentnews.com2018/03/23.

42. Bret Stephens, "Free Speech and the Necessity of Discomfort," *New York Times,* February 2, 2018.

tors' demands. How the University responded in light of its earlier position about free speech provides some historical context about how these issues have evolved in American higher education.

Some student demonstrators demanded that a Yale administrator, Erika Christakis, associate master of Silliman College, be sanctioned for insensitivity because she questioned whether the University should set rules about Halloween costumes. She had written:

> Even if we could agree on how to avoid offense—and I'll note no one around campus seems to be concerned about the offense taken by religiously conservative folks to skin-revealing costumes—I wonder, and I am not trying to be provocative: Is there no room anymore for a child or a young person to be a little bit obnoxious. . . a little bit inappropriate or, yes, offensive?[43]

She continued:

> American universities were once a safe space not only for maturation but also for a certain regressive, or even transgressive experience; increasingly it seems they have become places of censure and prohibition. And the censure and prohibition comes from above, not from yourselves! Are we all okay with this transfer of power? Have we lost faith in young people's capacity—in your capacity—to exercise self-censure, through social norming, and also in your capacity to ignore or reject things that trouble you?[44]

On November 9, about 1,000 Yale student demonstrators marched behind a banner that proclaimed, "WE OUT HERE. WE'VE BEEN HERE. WE AIN'T LEAVING. WE ARE LOVED." The rally ended with music and dancing.[45] Then the mood became sharper. On November 12, a coalition

---

43. The Christakis email was written on October 30, 2016.

44. Ibid.

45. The *Yale Alumni Magazine* which had just become an official University publication published a lengthy description of these events by Kathrin Day Lassila'81 "Race, speech and values: What really happened at Yale," Jan/Feb 2016. Pp.41–50. An extensive section of letters and comments was published in the March/April 2016 of that magazine. See also, Sarah Brown, "At Yale, Painful Rifts Emerge Over Diversity and Free Speech," *The Chronicle of Higher Education,* October, 2016.

of about 200 students, mostly undergraduate women of color, marched at midnight to Yale President Salovey's house and presented him with a list of demands that included ". . . removal of the Christakises as master and associate master, increased funding for cultural centers, an ethnic studies distributional requirement for all undergraduates, mental health counseling at all cultural centers, and more resources for low income students."[46]

Conflict often causes a centralization of power in governments, corporations, and universities. Yale's top administrators did not consider the matter of possible offensive Halloween costumes an appropriate matter for debate or a learning experience for the whole campus. Instead they sought administratively to manage the situation by top-down statements and assuring the protesters of their empathy toward them.

In his November public response to the Yale community campus about the costume controversy, President Peter Salovey first declared:

> We cannot overstate the importance we put on our community's diversity, and the need to increase it, support it, and respect it. We know we have work to do, for example in increasing the diversity of our faculty and the initiatives taken last week move us closer to that goal. We are proud of the diversity on our campus and the vibrant communities at the Afro-Am House, the Asian American Cultural Center, La Casa Cultural and the Native American Cultural Center. We are proud to support our lesbian, gay, bisexual, transgender and queer students, staff and faculty. We are proud to support women. And we are proud to attract students and scholars from around the world, of all faiths and traditions, and with all levels of physical ability. We are committed to supporting all of these communities, not only by attending to their safety and well-being but in the expectation they will be treated with respect.[47]

President Salovey did not concede that the priority traditionally given to freedom of speech had been downgraded. Indeed, he hyperlinked to the University's 1974 Woodward report, named after its chair the distin-

---

46. Lassilla, p. 44.

47. Peter Salovey, "An Update from the Campus, November, 2016. There is a line between affirming various forms of preexisting diversity among students and promoting tribalism. It is not certain in President Salovey's statement that he has found it.

guished historian C. Vann Woodward. That committee of faculty from various schools and other constituencies was appointed by President Kingman Brewster after a series of controversies over whether Governor George Wallace, General William Westmoreland, Secretary of State William Rogers, and Professor William Shockley, among others, would be permitted to speak on campus in the face of student and community protests.

The Committee reached a consensus that:

The primary function of a university is to discover and disseminate knowledge by means of research and teaching. To fulfill this function a free exchange of ideas is necessary not only within its walls but with the world beyond as well. It follows that the university must do everything possible to ensure within the fullest degree of intellectual freedom. The history of intellectual growth and discovery clearly demonstrates the need for unfettered freedom, the right to think the unthinkable, discuss the unmentionable, and challenge the unchallengeable. To curtail free expression strikes twice at intellectual freedom, for whomever deprives another of the right to state unpopular views necessarily also deprives others of the right to listen to those views.

For if the university is a place for knowledge, it is also a special kind of small society. Yet it is not primarily a fellowship, a club, a circle of friends, a replica of civil society around it. Without sacrificing its central purpose, it cannot make its primary and dominant value the fostering of friendship, solidarity, harmony, civility, or mutual respect. To be sure, these are important values: other institutions may properly assign them the highest, and not merely a subordinate priority, and a good university will seek and may in some significant measure attain these ends. But it will never let these values, important as they are, override its central purpose. We value freedom of expression precisely because it provides a forum for the new, the provocative, the disturbing, and the unorthodox. Free speech is the barrier to the tyranny of authoritarian or even majority opinion as to rightness or wrongness of particular doctrines or thoughts.[48]

---

48. "Report of the Committee on Freedom of Expression at Yale" was issued December 22, 1974.

There was one dissenter to the Committee report, Kenneth J. Barnes, an economics graduate student who in many ways expressed presciently the contemporary arguments for suppressing speech. He argued "that all knowledge is relative, the result of social conditioning." He quoted Herbert Marcuse and Yale Chaplain, William Sloan Coffin, who declared. "Unless social justice is established in a country, civil liberties which always concern intellectuals more than social justice, look like luxuries." Mr. Barnes concluded that "If democratic, undominated discussion within the community so determines, we may prohibit the malicious advocacy of racist or imperialist ideas." He agreed that "free expression is an important value, but it is not the only value which we uphold, either in our society or in our universities. Under certain circumstances, free expression is outweighed by more pressing issues, including liberation of all oppressed peoples and equal opportunities for minority groups."[49]

In some respects in the modern university, graduate student Barnes' perspective has overwhelmed the faculty heavyweights on the Woodward Committee as the actions Yale took toward empathizing with sensitivities of various groups show.

But there was some fallout. Without commenting on President Salovey's letters to the Yale community, except to agree with his decision not to fire Silliman College's Master and Associate Master, Nicholas and Erika Christakis, 46 Yale Professors signed a letter affirming their belief in freedom of speech. They wrote:

> Free speech of course includes the right to express opinions that are opposed to what may be termed liberal or progressive values, but that is not the issue in the current situation. We are deeply troubled that this modest attempt to ask people to consider the issue of self-monitoring vs. bureaucratic supervision has been misinterpreted, and in some cases recklessly distorted, as support for racist speech and hence as justification for demanding the resignation of our colleagues from their posts at Silliman.[50]

---

49. Ibid.

50. Scott Jaschik, "Yale professors issue an open letter on free speech," *Inside Higher Education*, December 1, 2015.

The professors went on to state: "While the university stands for many values, none is more central than freedom of speech. . . A crucial component of free expression is the possibility of open and civil disagreement, without vilifying those who disagree with one's own viewpoint." The signers concluded that they all agreed that Yale needed to further diversify its faculty, staff, administration, and student body and that the Christakis's had done good work for social justice in the past. Later some 700 students, faculty, staff, and alumni affixed their signatures to that letter.[51] Nevertheless, one student looking at the signatories commented to the *Yale Daily News*, "Hey at least now we have a catalogue of professors we should never take classes with."

Erika Christakis subsequently decided that although "I have great respect and affection for my students, I worry that the current climate at Yale is not in my view, conducive to the civil dialogue and open inquiry required to solve our urgent societal problems." Consequently, she said she could no longer teach at the University. She has maintained her administrative position.[52] The Yale administration has insisted that she was not pressured by it to alter her university responsibilities.[53]

In the end, Yale had a very widespread intense discussion about race. It was almost impossible to avoid, given campus attitudes, and the national spotlight. There was no violence or even sit-ins of administrative spaces, but the discourse focused almost exclusively on feelings. Facts about

---

51. Lassilla, p.44.

52. Scott Jaschik, "Academic at center of Yale controversy over Halloween costumes won't teach there again," *Inside Higher Education,* December 7, 2015. See also, Connor Friedersdorf, "The Perils of Writing a Provocative Email at Yale, " *The Atlantic,* May 26, 2016.

For another perspective about the Yale controversies, see Daniel W. Drezner, "The trouble with 21st Century campus politics," *The Washington Post,* November 9, 2015. He points to the role the Christakises had as administrators of a residence hall, but he also includes a video of the Yale undergraduate demanding the University provide her with a "safe space," swearing at Nicholas Christakis and ending by saying, "I don't want to debate. I want to talk about my pain." For a full quote of the invectives hurled at Christakis see Ollie Gillman, "The Moment Yale Students Encircled and Shouted Down Professor Who Told Them to Just 'Look Away' if They Were Offended by Halloween Customs," *Daily Mail,* November 7, 2015 as quoted by Sykes, *Fail U,* p.186. For a more extended view of Nicholas Christakis' views on speech see his *New York Times* essay, "Teaching Inclusion in a Divided World," June 22, 2016, "And so the faculty must cut to the root of a set of ideas that are wholly illiberal. Disagreement is not oppression, Argument is not assault. Words—even provocative or repugnant ones—are not violence. The answer to speech we do not like is more speech."

53. Lassilla, p.47.

trends in admission and hiring policies, budgetary allocations, and events programming at the University seemed almost irrelevant. There did not appear to be any serious attempt to document actual discrimination on campus. There was no organized debate about institutional realities.[54] President Salovey concluded after one of his meetings that "to have about 50 minority students in a room with me saying to me that their experience was not what they hoped it would be—I take personal responsibility for that and I consider it a failure."[55]

The "we believe in academic freedom, but students are our customers," conflict was also in evidence at Vanderbilt University in 2015. Carol Swain, Professor of Political Science and Law, wrote an op-ed in Nashville's major paper titled "Charlie Hebdo attacks prove critics were right about Islam." In it she asks, "What would it take to make us admit we were wrong about Islam?"[56] Sometimes she criticized "radical" Islam; sometimes just Islam.

She made no reference to anything on the Vanderbilt campus. Nevertheless, more than 1500 Vanderbilt students and alumni signed an on-line petition originally asking for her suspension and requiring additional diversity training, though the final version was amended in a nodding deference to her freedom of speech. Vanderbilt's Chancellor Nicholas S. Zeppos eventually weighed in on the controversy. He did not suggest that the role of Islam in the world be debated, speakers be invited, or that any other

---

54. When the William F. Buckley, Jr. program at Yale attempted to have a forum on campus free speech in response to the Halloween controversy, the event was disrupted and speakers harassed. Monica Wang, Joey Ye, and Victor Wang, "Students Protest Buckley Talk," *Yale Daily News,* November 9, 2015. The program also sponsors an annual dinner honoring disinvited or harassed campus speakers. In 2019, it will feature Henry Kissinger who was interrupted, while trying to speak at New York University on the 45 year anniversary of his being awarded the Nobel Peace Prize. Sarah Jackson and Victor Porcelli, "Henry Kissinger Told to 'Rot in Hell.' Disrupted Four Times During Talk at Stern," October 16, 2018. news@nyu.com. In 2017, the Yale Buckley program using McLaughlin & Associates surveyed 872 Yale undergraduates and found there was overwhelming support for intellectual diversity and opposition to speech codes, but many felt intimidated to share their ideas in class. Republicans were about twice as likely as Democrats to feel intimidation, though a majority of moderates agreed. www.mclaughlinonline.com.

55. Lassilla, p.47. In 2018, Yale made Nicholas Christakis a Sterling Professor, one of its highest academic honors, and Jamie Kirchik, opposed to the way the Yale administration handled the Halloween controversy and other issues, ran an anti-establishment campaign to be elected a member of the University's Board of Trustee's. See his article, "Reflections on the Revolution at Yale," *Quillette,* September 9, 2018.

56. *Tennessean,* January 14, 2015.

educational programs be initiated. He did not describe or discuss any of Swain's specific ideas. Instead he wrote:

> I have heard and appreciate the serious concerns of our students and alumni who have signed an on-line petition calling for the suspension of Carol Swain... Professor Swain's opinions are her own. They do not reflect the opinions of the university in any way. They are not my opinions, the opinions of the provost, or the opinions of the university leadership.[57]

Unless the Vanderbilt faculty are unusually quiescent, the University's leadership does not take pains to dissociate itself every time a professor writes a controversial op-ed. What appeared to have motivated Chancellor Zeppos was evident in what he said following his disassociation: "Ensuring that our campus is a safe, welcoming place and supportive environment for every member of the Vanderbilt community has been and always will be our top priority." He conceded that freedom of speech is important at Vanderbilt, even if the expressions may be of unpopular or offensive views, but he added: "However speech whose sole purpose or effect is to discriminate, stigmatize, retaliate, offend, foment hatred or violence, or cause harm has no place in this university." But if speech that has the "effect" of offending someone has no legitimate academic role, then could a professor safely compare sharia law to the Bill of Rights or the 14th Amendment or for that matter discuss any topic relating to religion in a classroom or an op-ed? Would the answer depend on whether those offended created an on-line petition demanding sanctions for the offensive speech and speaker?[58]

Another instance of an administrator publicly rejecting a faculty viewpoint occurred at the University of Pennsylvania Law School, this time with real curriculum consequences. Amy Wax, Robert Mundheim Professor of Law, believes that one of the reasons that African-American students fall behind in academic pursuits is cultural.[59] When such students are admit-

---

57. http://news.vanderbilt-university-suspend-professor-carol-swain/u14139398 (1/24/2015).

58. In March 2017, Professor Swain announced her early retirement from Vanderbilt. Marc Parry, "A Christian Conservative Professor Accuses Colleges of Indoctrinating Students," *The Chronicle of Higher Education*, March 19, 2017.

59. Amy L. Wax, "Educating the Disadvantaged—Two Models," *Harvard Journal of Law and Public Policy*, Vol. 40, No 3. (2017), pp.686–728. See also, Amy Wax, "The University of

ted to highly selective law schools, they are unlikely to perform well in the class ranking law schools do. Her published views have been vigorously criticized, but her remarks about the absence of black students in the top of UPenn class rankings in a videotaped interview with Brown Professor Glenn Loury caused the Penn Chapter of the National Lawyers Guild to call for her dismissal. Law School Dean, Ted Ruger disowned her views and claimed that her generalization about class ranking was empirically wrong, though he refused to release any data supporting any conclusion pro or con. He then removed Professor Wax from a class teaching first year students.

Many universities no longer behave as though their top priority is "to discover and disseminate knowledge" in the language of the Woodward report. Such a goal may be a particular faculty priority, but in the post-modern era even some professors have come to believe there is no such thing as objective truth. Further discovering knowledge is not a priority for a university's Office of Student Affairs, its Office of Institutional Advancement, and certainly not what is the largest department at many universities, Athletics. Trustees may be interested in knowledge that can be patented or serves some important economic stakeholders, but they must also be concerned about endowment returns, enrollment trends, and liability issues. Presidents must focus on what concerns their trustees, their institution's rankings, and media image. In the exceptionally competitive environment of American education, unspoken priorities for many institutions are a relentless pursuit of status and money. Their public role, many on and off campus would argue, is serving a state's or local community's political agendas. Others would give priority to creating social justice with its emphasis on diversity, inclusion, and tolerance, while also seeking to overturn the established social order. In none of those hidden or open goals is robust free speech or frequent debates on controversial subjects seen as an asset, let alone a necessity. In the modern university, the boundaries between acceptable criticism and student well-being are always determined subjectively, usually after administrative intervention, following instructions by the "communities" of "marginalized" groups in President Salovey's list.

There are substantial incentives for protest for these groups. After Yale promised to keep them safe and comfortable, President Salovey noted, "Race, ethnicity, and other aspects of social identity are central issues of our era, issues that should be a focus of particularly intense study at a great

Denial," *The Wall Street Journal*, March 22, 2018.

university." Consequently, the University had earlier committed a budget of $50 million to be spent on growing "faculty diversity," creating a deputy dean for diversity, greatly increasing the budget of the four race and ethnic cultural centers, training for all administrators "on recognizing and combatting racism and other forms of discrimination in the academy," and changing the orientation programs to stress inclusion. The budgets of the Afro-Am House, the Asian American Cultural Center, La Casa Cultural, and the Native American Cultural Center were to be doubled in the 2016–17 university budget.[60]

In the spring of 2017, incidents on both coasts demonstrated how intolerant some students can be when speakers are invited whose past writing they found to be disagreeable. The most publicized was at Middlebury College where Charles Murray was invited by a campus student group to speak about the implications of his recent book "Coming Apart," a work highly relevant to the outcome of the 2016 national election. When he began to speak, some in the audience of students and faculty not only turned their backs on him, but created such a tumult that the event had to be moved to a more secure location and livestreamed. As Murray and Middlebury Professor of Political Science and moderator, Allison Stanger, left the lecture hall she was assaulted and injured.[61] Professor Stanger later wrote "A majority of faculty and students are progressive. A small minority are conservative; many of them are in the closet, afraid to speak their minds for fear of being denounced as reactionary bigots."[62] Later a letter signed by almost 100 Middlebury professors proclaimed: "Genuine higher learning is possible only where free, reasoned and civil speech and discussion are respected. No group of professors or students has the right to determine for the entire

---

60. Peter Salovey, "Toward a Better Yale," November 17, 2015.

61. Scott Jaschik, "Middlebury students shout down lecture by Charles Murray," "Middlebury engages in soul-searching after speech is shouted down and professor is attacked." "Middlebury president vows 'accountability' for those who disrupted lecture and attacked professor." *Inside Higher Education.* March 3, 6 and 7, 2017. In support of the protest tactics, see John Patrick Leahy, "A defense of the student protest of Charles Murray's speech at Middlebury College." *Inside Higher Education,* March 7, 2017. For Murray's view of the Middlebury events see, "Reflections on the Revolution at Middlebury." on the AEI website, March 7, 2017. There is, of course, a YouTube of the protest. "Students Protest Lecture by Charles Murray at Middlebury."

62. Middlebury: My Divided Campus," *New York Times,* April 2, 2017.

community that a question is closed for discussion."[63] Middlebury later disciplined about 68 students, though none were expelled.[64]

About a month later, some students at Claremont McKenna College protested a speech, to be followed by a question- and- answer period, by Heather MacDonald of the Manhattan Institute who had criticized the Black Lives Matter movement. Arguing that MacDonald's views were racist, about 170 students blocked the audience from hearing her speak. The College found that blockading the speech site "breached institutional values of freedom of expression and assembly" and suspended or put on probation five students.[65] These actions created their own blowback. Nana Gyamfi, a lawyer who had been advising the students and who was a part-time faculty member at Cal State University, Los Angeles teaching a course called Race, Activism and Emotions, argued the College was not really committed to diversity because, although it had created "a quota of marginalized people," it had not "created safe spaces for them where students feel respected." Furthermore, Gyamfi noted that the protestors did not grab MacDonald and pull her aside and declared that "there is no right to hear someone speak."

Up the coast at Reed College in Oregon, as student began the fall semester by taking the venerable Humanities 110 course, the faculty panelists were confronted by demonstrators who shouted, "We're protesting HUM 110 because it is Eurocentric." The previous year a dozen or so students occupied the 110 classroom waving cardboard signs, taping their mouths shut to protest the absence of non-white voices and in one instance taking over the class podium. When assistant professor Lucia Martinez Valdivia,

---

63. Chris Martin, "Free Inquiry on Campus: A Statement by a Collection of Middlebury Faculty," *The Heterodox Academy* website, March 7, 2017. See also "Middlebury: My Divided Campus" in which Professor Stanger concluded: "Upholding freedom of expression on college campuses is a necessary condition for sustaining constitutional democracy. As a unique experiment in transcending tribal allegiances, Americans are defined by the ideals we uphold together. What is "E pluribus unum but a brave and free space"?

64. Scott Jaschik, "Middlebury announces additional punishments related to disruption of Charles Murray lecture," *Inside Higher Education*, May 15, 2017. Murray's comments on putting these students on probation can be found at "Fecklessness at Middlebury," http://aei.org/publication/ fecklessness. . .

65. Scott Jaschik, "Claremont McKenna suspends 5 students for blocking a speech," *Inside Higher Education*, July 18, 2017. Two years earlier, Mary Spellman, the Dean of Students at the College was forced to resign after student protests and hunger strikes claiming she was insensitive. One hundred faculty members signed a letter supporting the protests. The College President then created two new positions focused on "diversity."

who describes herself as queer and mixed race, tried to lecture on Sappho, she was berated as a "race traitor" upholding white supremacist principles for failing to oppose the 110 syllabus and as a "gaslighter" for "making disadvantaged students doubt their own oppression." Professor Valdivia, who presumably as an assistant was untenured, later wrote:

> I am intimidated by these students. I am scared to teach courses on race, gender or sexuality or even texts that bring these issues in any way. ... I'm at a loss as to how to begin to address it. Especially since many of these students don't believe in historicity or objective facts (they denounce the latter as being a tool of whitecisheteropatriarchy).[66]

Professor Valdivia's fears proved justified when a few weeks later, Kimberly Pierce, the gender fluid director of "Boys Don't Cry," a sympathetic portrayal of transgender persons, was invited to speak at Reed. Posters advertising the event were ripped down and Ms. Pierce was shouted down when she tried to speak. Dean of the Faculty, Nigel Nicholson later wrote that students came to the event "asking questions designed to indict the speaker. . . It felt like a courtroom, not a college." Ms. Pierce's alleged crime was casting Hillary Swank, a non-trans actor in the lead movie role.[67]

---

66. This quote and the description of Reed events comes largely from "Blue on blue," *The Economist*, September 9, 2017.

67. Another incident where a transgendered student felt "unsafe" because of a faculty lecture concerning child abuse occurred at the School of the Art Institute of Chicago. (SAIC) Professor Michael Bonesteel taught courses featuring comics where there is sometimes violence and other bizarre behavior, but did not use trigger warnings. SAIC investigated the complaint and reduced Bonesteel's teaching load to the point that he lost his insurance and resigned. The School responded to press stories by declaring: "We're an incredibly diverse school, we welcome all kinds of students and we want to make sure our environment is welcoming." Bonesteel appealed to the College Art Association and its executive director Hunter O'Hanian, who without taking a position on the particular case, was quoted as saying: "The problem comes when certain students feel challenged by hearing opposing ideas, or faculty members are challenged by hearing opposing those opposing ideas and they don't hear them as simply another point of view, but they hear them as trying to force another point of view. If people aren't safe to have a conversation on a college campus, then I don't know where they are able to be safe." Nick Roll, "Debate over art, teaching and prejudice at the School of the Art Institute of Chicago," *Inside Higher Education*, July 24, 2017. See also a report by F.I.R.E, "One Man's Vulgarity: Art censorship on American Campuses," 2018.

The most publicized incident on the West Coast involving freedom of speech and coercion occurred at Evergreen State College in Olympia, Washington. The College had a tradition of a "Day of Absence" when students and faculty "of color" left the campus to commune and demonstrate how enriched the campus is by their presence. In 2017, white faculty and students were also urged to cease their activities on the "Day," April 12. Professor Bret Weinstein, who had no objection to the tradition, but did not believe he should be asked to call off his biology class and went ahead as scheduled. His nonconformity was noted and six weeks later 50 students invaded his class, shouting obscenities, calling him a racist and demanding his resignation. Perhaps because they were told to "stand down," campus police did not intervene. Unable to protect himself, Weinstein and his wife, Heather Heying, also a biology professor left the campus.[68]

Then the protestors took over the office of President George Bridges, screaming and swearing at him. Bridges was an odd target. After he was hired in 2015, he committed himself to focusing College policies on equity and social justice, with an emphasis on racial issues. An Equity Council was formed by Bridges and faculty were asked to sign a binary manifesto of support or opposition.[69]

These events at a small state campus of 4,300 students became a national and even international story and that did not end well for Evergreen.[70]

---

68. Professor Heying has described her experiences in "Life after Evergreen," 30 minute podcast. National Association of Scholars.

69. These events were very widely reported, An in-depth analysis can be found at Uri Harris, "How Activists Took Control of a University: The Case Study of Evergreen State." *Quillette*, December 22, 2017.

70. For a review of these events from the College's perspective, see the minutes of the Evergreen Board of Trustees, March 12, 2018 and the April 1, 2018 "Report of The Independent External Review Panel on the Evergreen College Response to the Spring 2017 campus events." The latter report pointed out that there were protests on many campuses that year, that Professor Weinstein appeared on Fox News, and that the video of the Evergreen student protests had gone viral. The report also noted that "as previously underrepresented populations grow and attend historically majority white institutions, colleges must adapt their teaching, learning, curriculum, and campus life to new realities and expectations across cultural differences." The report notes "Evergreen can no longer be considered a 'selective institution' in terms of admission, with an admit rate that exceeds 95%." (p.15) The percentage of 'students of color," particularly Hispanics has greatly increased and that 60% of first year full time students identified as LGBTQUIA. Evergreen's graduation rate ranked 6th among Washington State's campuses.

Weinstein and Heying, filed a $3.8 million Tort Claim against the College. Despite an increased legislative appropriation for its campus police, for 2018, Evergreen was faced with a $5.9 million dollar deficit and had to cut 10 percent from its operating budget, leading to staff reductions, and tuition increases.[71] By the fall of 2018, only 300 new freshmen showed up and the total enrollment was down to 2800.

Across the country again at the College of William & Mary, Clair Guthrie Gastanaga, Executive Director of the ACLU Virginia chapter, was prevented from giving a talk on free speech by students claiming to represent the Black Lives Matter movement. They shouted her down by chanting, "ACLU, Free Speech for who? The oppressed are not impressed. ACLU, you protect Hitler too. Blood is on your hands. Free speech hides beneath white sheets."

These actions clearly violated the College's student code of conduct and President Taylor Reveley III declared: "We do not want any event to be ended early or shut down because someone disagrees with the views of the speaker or is attempting to prevent speech and questions by those attending. We must be a campus that welcomes difficult conversations, honest debate and civil dialogue."[72]

---

71. Abby Spegman, "Evergreen looks to cut $6 million from its budget, raise fees due to enrollment drop." *The Olympian,* March 5, 2018.

72. Jeremy Bauer-Wolf, "William & Mary students who shut down ACLU event broke student code," *Inside Higher Education,* October 6, 2017. The ACLU response was "We also support the goals espoused by the demonstrators (ending white supremacy, achieving racial justice and elevating those who have been oppressed). It is more than disappointing, however, when robust debate that should be the hallmark of the cult(sic) of inquiry on a college campus is disrupted by those who seek with their own voices or act simply to silence others who took actions or hold views on principles with which [they] disagree." https://acluva.org//en/news/aclu-va-statement-regarding-sept 27-event.

A year later, the ACLU was engulfed in an internal policy debate about the priority of free speech when it might appear to conflict with racial justice goals. See Wendy Kaminer, "The ACLU Retreats From Free Expression," *The Wall Street Journal,* June 20, 2018. She pointed to new ACLU guidelines, emanating from the organization's fundraising and communications personal, suggesting that factors in taking a case such as its potential effects on "marginalized communities" and on the ACLU's "credibility" should be weighed. For further insight into ACLU's policies see The Volokh Blog, https://Reason.com/volokh/2018/06/22/aclus-DavidColeresponds. For a comprehensive description of the recent growth of the ACLU and its change in priorities see Marin Cogan, "The Twilight of Free Speech Liberalism," *The New Republic,* July 16, 2018. Whatever the reason, the fact is that the ACLU has

Protestors also disrupted speeches by the Presidents of Virginia Tech University and the University of Oregon in opening fall 2017 semester convocations.[73] In the spring of 2018, an undergraduate organization called "People's State of the University" at Duke University disrupted President Vincent Price's speech celebrating alumni donations to the institution. The protestors wanted a $15 minimum wage and hiring persons of specific ethnicities and sexual orientations. Rushing the stage, the protestors shouted for President Price to get off and silenced him. After the Office of Student Conduct opened an inquiry into the alumni affair, more than 100 Duke faculty signed a letter urging no discipline for the protestors and the investigation was closed. It was an awkward moment for the University. In 2015–16, alumni giving set a record of $571 million in gifts and pledges.[74]

It is not just speeches that are suppressed, but also theatrical performances.[75] At Knox College, the theater department planned to stage Bertolt Brecht's "The Good Person of Szechwan" which asks the question whether a person can be good, if the world isn't. Some students protested and the Knox student newspaper agreed with their objections in an op-ed:

> The theatre department is a very white department—like many departments at Knox—and needs to acknowledge that they are coming from a place of privilege and prejudice. They need to listen to their students when they voice their concerns about not only the plays the department produces, but about interactions with insensitive faculty and problematic syllabi.[76]

The play was canceled and Elizabeth Carlin-Metz, Smith V. Brand Endowed Chair of Theater Arts, commented:

---

been largely absent from the disinvitation and disruption campus speech controversies. That role has been filled by F.I.R.E, and other organizations.

73. Nick Roll, "As speaker interruptions continue, controversial policy adopted in Wisconsin," *Inside Higher Education*, October 9, 2017.

74. Anne Hendershott, "Are Alumni Pulling the Policy in Academia?" *Minding The Campus,* June 11, 2018.

75. Brandeis University also called off a play about comedian Lenny Bruce, after students and faculty expressed concern about how the play treated race. The play was later given off campus in a professional venue.

76. Colleen Flaherty, "Knox College calls off Brecht play after complaints of racial insensitivity," Inside Higher Education, November 10, 2017.

Given the level of emotions at the moment, we felt that the teaching moment was lost, and that we'd move toward creating a teaching envelope around these kinds of issues. How do you prepare students to deal with difficult texts, and basically lay the groundwork for addressing a play that is from a time when there were other standards —standards which today we would find racist or sexist or any of those things? And how do we not eliminate our history?[77]

The idea of giving the play and then debating its values and casting was apparently not considered.

Looking back, these incidents were episodic in the larger scale of American higher education, but, nevertheless, they may have cast a much wider chilling effect and created considerable public skepticism about the state of academic freedom in the United States.[78] It may be the real culprit was not a few activist responses to particular speakers, newspaper articles or plays, but an overall failure to create a culture of debate on campuses.

B. Constitutional Law

All public educational institutions are bound by federal court decisions about the scope of the First Amendment which as this section will show is expansive. While private higher education is not bound by the First Amendment's free speech requirements, it is unlikely that any selective, secular campus would concede that it has less commitment to freedom of speech than state institutions which must follow constitutional rules. If so, its stated commitment may constitute a contractual obligation to respect

---

77. Ibid.

78. See Matt Grossman and David A. Hopkins, "How the conservative movement has undermined trust in higher education," *Inside Higher Education,*" October 11, 2016. Their essay does not discuss the free speech issues recorded in this research.

dissenting speech.[79] The test of the expanse of freedom of speech is always at the margins, the hard cases.[80]

At least regarding public institutions, judicial priorities for protecting freedom of speech are different than the "reputation and comfort" versus "freedom" balancers controlling many contemporary campus policies.[81] Federal courts have been particularly concerned to protect an open intellectual atmosphere on campus. In 1967, the Supreme Court in *Keyishian* declared:

> To impose any strait jacket upon intellectual leaders in our colleges and universities would imperil the future of our nation. No field of education is so thoroughly comprehended by man that new discoveries cannot yet be made. Particularly is that true in the social sciences where few, if any principles are accepted as absolutes. Scholarship cannot flourish is an atmosphere of suspicion and distrust. Teachers and students must always be free to inquire, to study and to evaluate, to

---

79. See also *John McAdams v. Marquette University*, July 6, 2018 where the Wisconsin Supreme Court overturned the Jesuit university's decision to suspend Prof. McAdams without pay for his blog comments criticizing an instructor/graduate student for curtailing speech criticizing same sex marriage. Its faculty handbook states: "Academic freedom is prized as essential to Marquette University and to its living growth as a university." It then adopted verbatim much of the AAUP guidelines on academic freedom as have many private universities. The AAUP, though, filed an amicus brief on McAdams' behalf. NAS also filed an amicus brief on behalf of McAdams and Peter Wood, its executive director, served as his expert witness. For a lengthy description of the case and multiple comments, see Colleen Flaherty, "Divided Wisconsin Supreme Court Backs Marquette Faculty Blogger," *Inside Higher Education*, July 9, 2018.

80. For comprehensive book length views of free speech law, see Eugene Volokh, *The First Amendment* (New York: Foundation Press, 2013) and Randy Robinson, *Free Speech on America's K-12 and College Campuses* (Lanham, MD: Lexington Books, 2016), and Erwin Chemerinsky and Howard Gillian (New Haven, Ct.: Yale University Press, 2016). See also, George Leef, "The 'Right' to Disrupt Free Speech on Campus Doesn't Exist," The James G. Martin Center, January 3, 2018.

81. For an historical review of this subject see Henry Gates, Jr. ed. *Speaking of Race; Speaking of Sex; Hate Speech, Civil Rights and Civil Liberties* (New York: New York University Press, 1994); Samuel Walker, *Hate Speech: The History of an American Controversy* (Lincoln, NE: University of Nebraska Press, 1994) and Lawrence R. Marcus, *Fighting Words: The Politics of Hate Speech* (New York: Praeger, 1996).

gain new maturity and understanding, otherwise our civilization will stagnate and die.[82]

The threat in the *Keyishian* and *Sweezy* cases was from off-campus state government censors, but courts have also applied these principles when the censors were on-campus administrators or students. In 1972, the Supreme Court unanimously struck down a decision by Central Connecticut State College not to certify a student chapter of Students for a Democratic Society for use of campus spaces, ostensibly on the grounds that their national organization might engage in violence. Justice Powell wrote:

> Yet the precedents of this Court leave no room for the view that, because of the acknowledged need for order, First Amendment protections should apply with less force on college campuses than in the community at large. Quite the contrary. '[t]he vigilant protection of constitutional freedom is nowhere more vital than in the community of American schools.' *Shelton v. Tucker*, 364 U.S. 479,364 (1960). "The college classroom with its surrounding environs, is peculiarly the *'marketplace of ideas,' and we break no new constitutional ground in affirming the Nation's dedication to safeguarding academic freedom.*" (emphasis in the original)[83]

For similar reasons, that is why speech codes when they are challenged rarely survive judicial review.[84]

The Supreme Court has considered the obligation of authorities to protect speech, even when it might disturb members of local communities who sought to suppress speech with which they disagreed. When a suspended Catholic priest attempted to give a speech praising fascist leaders, criticizing some American public officials, and making anti-Semitic remarks, persons outside the rented auditorium clashed with the audience inside. Chicago police were unable to keep order and the speaker was fined

---

82. *Keyishian v. Board of Regents,* 385 U.S.589 (1967) quoting *Sweezy v. New Hampshire,* 354 U.S. 234,250 (1957).

83. *Healy v. James,* 408 U.S.169, 180 (1972).

84. *Doe v. University of Michigan* (1989); *UWM Post Inc. v. Board of Regents of the University of Wisconsin System* (1991); *Iota Xi Chapter of Sigma Chi Fraternity v. George Mason University* (1991); *Curry v. Stanford University* (1995) and *Cohen v. San Bernardino College* (1996).

$100 for violation of the city's breech of the peace law. In its 1949 landmark decision on the Heckler's Veto in *Terminiello v. Chicago,* the Court placed the responsibility on government to protect speakers, holding that:

> The State's position, therefore, amounts to a claim that an audience that takes serious offense at particular expression is likely to disturb the peace and that expression may be prohibited on that basis. Our precedents do not countenance such a presumption. On the contrary, they recognize that a principal function of free speech under our system of government is to invite dispute. It may indeed best serve its high purpose when it induces a condition of unrest, creates dissatisfaction with conditions as they are or even stirs people to anger.[85]

There is a more modern form of Heckler's Veto on some campuses. If an invited speaker is thought to be "controversial," more than normal security may be needed and the student organization sponsor may be asked to pay for this added protection. The problem is that off-campus or student activists opposed to the speaker may issue threats thus requiring extra security and creating a "tax" on the right to speak and to listen.[86] When the student chapters of College Republicans and Young America's Foundation at the University of California, Berkeley believed their campus was imposing more security costs and other impediments to bringing in their speakers, they brought a lawsuit in 2017 claiming the University's policy gave unfettered discretion to administrators to control who and when outside speakers could appear.[87] On January 25, 2018, the U.S. Department of Justice filed a formal "Statement of Interest" in the case stating that, if the facts alleged were true, Berkeley's policies violated the First Amendment

---

85. 337 U.S.1, 4.

86. Several institutions enacted such policies after events such as occurred in Berkeley where masked protesters committed arson and vandalism to object to a speech by Milo Yiannopolis and the University and City police appeared to "stand down." University authorities then canceled the speech.

87. Scott Jaschik, "Justice Dept. Backs Suit Against Berkeley," *Inside Higher Education,* January 26, 2018. UC Berkeley did realize it had a problem and has adopted more proactive policies to foster rational debate on policy issues and to lessen interest in more provocative speakers. Jeremy Bauer-Wolf, "Civility at Berkeley," *Inside Higher Education,* November 28, 2018.

by creating prior restraint of speech.[88] The University settled the case by making a substantial payment to the plaintiffs without acknowledging any wrongdoing.

On June 18, 2018, the University of Washington settled a case involving $17,000 in security fees imposed on the UW Republican club which wanted to sponsor a rally for a group called Patriot Prayer. Twenty-three UW law professors, including its former dean, asked the University to settle the case, pointing out that these fees could have the "effect of squelching unpopular views."[89] The University did not back off, however, until the day before the scheduled rally, when U.S. District Court Judge, Marsha Pechman issued a temporary restraining order finding that the fee setting guidelines were inconsistent with the First Amendment and could have the effect of chilling speech. UW, then, had to pay the students' legal advisors $122,000.

In *R.A.V. v. St. Paul* (1992), the Court confronted the most obnoxious and intimidating form of speech, a cross burning in a black family's fenced-in back yard. The justices unanimously held the City's ordinance unconstitutional either because it was content specific or overbroad. "The First Amendment does not permit St. Paul to impose special prohibitions on those speakers who express views on disfavored subjects."[90] In 2003, however, in *Virginia v. Black*, the Court held that, if there were a specific intent to intimidate, cross burning could not be justified, although such symbolic actions to express general ideological positions or group solidarity were protected.[91]

During the height of the Vietnam War, there were many protests, some peaceful, some not. In 1969, the Court examined the scope of free speech

---

88. U.S. Department of Justice Statement of Interest, Young America's Foundation and Berkley College Republicans v. Janet Napolitano, No.3:17-cv-02255-MMC. A comprehensive analysis of the law and problems campuses face when controversial speakers are invited can be found in Suzanne B, Goldberg, "Free Expression on Campus: Mitigating the Cost of Contentious Speakers," *Harvard Journal of Law and Public Policy,* Vol. 41, No 1, (Winter, 2018) Golding is Herbert and Doris Wechsler Clinical Professor of Law, Columbia Law School, and concludes that on balance that allowing "contentious speech" is the best policy, even at private universities where the First Amendment is not at issue.

89. Katherine Long, "UW to pay $122,500 in legal fees in settlement with College Republicans over free speech," *Seattle Times,* June 18, 2018.

90. 505 U.S. 377.

91. 538 U.S. 343.

rights that might disturb, even in public school settings. In *Tinker v. Des Moines*, the Court declared:

> The District Court concluded that the action of the school authorities was reasonable because it was based upon their fear of a disturbance from wearing [anti-war] armbands. But in our system, undifferentiated fear or apprehension of disturbance. . . . is not enough to overcome freedom of expression. Any departure from absolute regimentation may cause trouble. Any variation from the majority's opinion may inspire fear. Any words spoken in class, in the lunchroom or on the campus, that deviate from the views of another person, may start an argument or cause a disturbance. But our Constitution says we must take that risk; and our history says that it is this sort of hazardous freedom—this kind of openness—that is the basis of the independence and vigor of Americans who grow up and live in this relatively permissive, often disputative society.[92]

The Supreme Court, in *Rosenberger v. University of Virginia* (1995), ruled that the First Amendment requires that public higher education must be viewpoint neutral in financing student publications because:

> The quality and creative power of student intellectual life to this day remain a measure of a school's influence and attainment. For the University [of Virginia], by its regulations to cast disapproval on particular viewpoints of its students risks the suppression of free speech and creative inquiry in one of the vital centers of the Nation's intellectual life, its college and university campuses.[93]

The most common campus "disapproval of particular viewpoints" is to label any type of expression as "hate" speech that criticizes or demeans some group or the policies connected with that group.[94] These kinds of

---

92. 393 U.S. 505, 508.

93. 515 U.S. 819, 836.

94. "Hate speech" has been in society for a long time, but efforts to make it illegal in the United States, unlike other countries, are fairly recent. For example, C. Edwin Baker, Nicholas F. Galliocchio Professor of Law at the University of Pennsylvania, does not even discuss the concept in his 1989 book, *Human Liberty and Freedom of Speech* (New York: Oxford University Press).

regulations are distinct from the "fighting words" doctrine in which the Supreme Court found that face-to-face delivery of invectives were not protected speech.[95] Instead prohibitions of "hate speech" are used to justify shouting down lecturers, condemning editorials or penalizing generalized political commentary that some find offensive. Naturally academic administrators prefer campus atmospheres that are welcoming and even tranquil.[96]

After some unknown person chalked "deport" and "build a wall" on campus sidewalks, President Wallace Loh of the University of Maryland College Park responded that, many "young men and women at UMD and elsewhere are questioning where free speech ends and hate speech begins." President Loh went on to say that "Surely when wielded as a weapon hate speech does not deserve constitutional protection." He pointed out that UMD had:

> policies in place that protect undocumented students to the full extent the law permits. We have retained staff to support them and invited volunteer attorneys to advise them. . . . We allocated $100,000 for additional diversity and inclusion programming to benefit all members of the UMD community. We will deploy a trained rapid-response team in any hate-bias incident in order to provide support to any UMD member who is subject of such an incident.[97]

President Loh, who has a law degree and served as a law dean, did not discuss what kinds of expression about illegal immigration are legitimate at UMD.

The judiciary is more protective of free speech that can be labeled "hate speech." In a 2010 case, *David Rodriguez et.al v Maricopa County Community College*, the Ninth Circuit had to decide whether a faculty member's emails to the college community arguably demeaning Hispanics violated the College's obligation to create a workplace free of written harassment

---

95. *Chaplinsky v. New Hampshire,* 315 U.S. 568 (1942). A Jehovah's Witnesses pamphleteer called an inquiring policeman "a God dammed racketeer" and "a dammed Fascist."

96. Nina Burleigh, "The Battle Against 'Hate Speech' on College Campuses Gives Rise to a Generation that Hates Speech," *Newsweek,* May 26, 2016.This cover story provides a general overview of anti-free speech trends together with some video excerpts.

97. Wallace M. Loh, "Racism, Extremism and Hate: UM president calls on all of us to fight such cancers in our body politic," *Baltimore Sun,* May 29, 2017.

under Title VII. Plaintiffs sued for failing to discipline a mathematics professor for criticizing La Raza, immigration, and multiculturalism, while lauding Western Civilization and Columbus Day. The Circuit panel, including retired Supreme Court Associate Justice Sandra Day O'Connor sitting by special designation, ruled the College could not discipline the professor even though his remarks were inconsistent with its diversity policy. In Chief Judge Alex Kozinski's words:

> The Constitution embraces such a heated exchange of views, even (perhaps especially) when they concern sensitive topics like race, where the risk of conflict and insult is high. Without the right to stand against society's most strongly-held convictions, the marketplace of ideas would decline into a boutique of the banal, as the urge to censor is greatest where debate is most unquieting and orthodoxy is most entrenched. The right to provoke, offend and shock lies at the core of the First Amendment.
>
> This is particularly so on college campuses. Intellectual advancement has traditionally progressed though discord and dissent, as a diversity of views ensures that ideas survive because they are correct, not because they are popular. Colleges and universities—sheltered from currents of popular opinion by tradition, geography, tenure and monetary endowments—have historically fostered that exchange. But that role in our society will not survive, if certain points of view may be declared beyond the pale.[98]

The most recent ruling by the Supreme Court on speech that can be perceived as disparaging group members was in *Matel v. Tam* (June 19, 2017). In that case, Mr. Tam was the lead singer for an Asian-American rock band that titled itself "The Slants" asserting that such a moniker would take the sting out of what otherwise was an ethnic slur. The United States Patent and Trade Office refused the band the trademark use of that name on the grounds of a provision in the Lanham Act of 1946 which forbade any trademark "which may disparage . . . persons, living or dead, institutions, beliefs or national symbols or bring them into contempt, or disrepute." If the trademark examiner found that a "substantial composite, although not necessarily a majority of the referenced group, would find that the

---

98. *Rodriquez v. Maricopa County Community College District*, (9th Cir. 2010).

proposed mark . . . . to be disparaging in the context of contemporary attitudes," then the burden would shift to the applicant to show that the proposed trademark is not disparaging. In short, akin to many campus policies, a group or segments of a group were given the right to control through patent law what was said about them in the public arena. Whether the Court was aware of the controversies over campus speech and whether that influenced the final opinion cannot be known, but some the opinion's language is certainly applicable.

Although there were two separate opinions each commanding the signatures of four justices, the Supreme Court was unanimous in striking down the disparagement clause because its enforcement would put the government in the role of engaging in viewpoint discrimination.

Justice Alito, writing for himself, Chief Justice Roberts, Justice Thomas and Justice Breyer concluded "Speech that demeans on the basis of race, ethnicity, gender, religion, age, disability, or any other similar ground is hateful, but the proudest boast of our free speech jurisprudence is that we protect the freedom to express 'the thought that we hate.'" The opinion written by Justice Kennedy, joined by Justices Ginsburg, Sotomayor, and Kagan, is in some ways even more applicable to campus speech controversies, especially where the concept of inclusion has become the dominant policy. Kennedy wrote:

> A subject that is first defined by content and then regulated by or censored by mandating only one sort of comments is not viewpoint neutral. To prohibit all sides from criticizing their opponents makes a law more viewpoint based, not less so. . . . The First Amendment viewpoint neutrality principle protects more than the right to identify with a particular side. It protects the right to create and present arguments for particular positions in particular ways, as the speaker choses. By mandating positivity, the law here, might silence dissent and distort the marketplace of ideas.

Commenting on the significance of the 2017 *Tam* decision, Fordham University Professor of Law, Hugh Hansen wrote that the Court unanimously affirmed the scope of free speech, even about the most controversial language because we live in a time where the marketplace of ideas is imperiled for Americans. He asserted:

... it is difficult to find any such marketplace today. Newspapers are in decline. Television news shows are divided ideologically, with viewers driven by confirmation bias. The Internet is primarily a gathering place for digital mobs ready to tar and feather those who hold opposing views. The rest of us have gathered not in the public square but in private groups to which admission is dependent upon adherence to politically correct orthodoxy. It is safe inside these groups, where shared views are sacrosanct and never have to withstand scrutiny. Opposing views are there too, but only to be mocked from a distance. In this environment, free speech is permitted for somebody with the same views but is distained when it comes to opposing ones. Political correctness is the new tribalism.[99]

In this environment, what is the role of higher education regarding debate over controverted public policies?

C. Campus Perspectives on Controversial Speech

Why have so many students in "the vital centers of Nation's intellectual life" concluded that disturbing speech must be suppressed or at least carefully circumscribed? It may be generational. The First Amendment Center's 2013 annual survey showed that only a quarter of those 46 years and older thought First Amendment protections were too robust, while nearly half of Americans under that age agreed with those who would restrict speech rights.[100] Two years later, the Pew Global Attitudes survey asked whether government should be able to prevent people from making "statements that are offensive to minority groups." Only 12% of people over 70 concurred, but 40% of millennials agreed.[101] In a 2016 Gallup Poll, nearly a

---

99. http:www.scotusblog/2017/06/symposium-important-free-speech.

100. First Amendment Center, "The State of the First Amendment-2103."

101. Ibid. The practical difficulties of reconciling free speech and the opinions of many contemporary students, particularly after an appearance by one of the several provocateurs circulating among campuses, can be seen in this case study of DePaul University by Beth McMurtrie, "How to Promote Free Speech Without Alienating Students?" *The Chronicle of Higher Education*, October 29. 2016. A18. Philip Alcabes has urged higher education be more sympathetic to student protests and that some ideas are too offensive to be voiced. "Our Idea of Tolerant Isn't," *The Chronicle of Higher Education*, October 21, 2016, B10.

majority of students agreed that the access of the news media should be restricted when protesters want to be left alone (48 percent); when students believe a reporter will be biased (49 percent); or when students want to tell the story themselves on social media.[102]

When Erwin Chemerinsky, dean of the U.C. Irvine law school, and Howard Gillman, the campus chancellor, taught a course on the history of free speech, they found that their first-year students were "skeptical of well-established precedents for the protection of offensive or hateful speech" and "not used to teachers who believed that learning could take place in an environment where students were made uncomfortable or were forced to reflect on disturbing topics or had their views challenged rather than always validated." On the other hand, based on this small sample, the teachers concluded: "This generation has a very strong and persistent instinct to protect others against hateful, discriminatory or intolerant speech, especially in educational settings."[103]

Even some legal scholars agree with the need to curtail speech about some policies.[104] **Perhaps these doubts about the benefits of free speech metastasize because campuses have lost the concept that learning about controversial policies occurs best in a culture of debate.** The Foundation for Individual Rights and Education (F.I.R E.) found in a 2010 report that more than 55% of the campuses surveyed had speech codes that prohibited speech that would otherwise be protected off campus by non-students.

There has been considerable national criticism for campus-based movements to censor or channel speech. After a number of well-publicized incidents, several universities have reaffirmed their abstract commitment to free speech which is after all what every American constitutionally enjoys.[105] In the fall of 2016, incoming students at the University of Chicago were sent a letter that stated: "You will find that we expect members of

---

102. "Free Expression on Campus: A Survey of U.S. College Students and U.S. Adults," Gallup, Inc., September 23, 2016.

103. "Free speech, Rebalanced," *The Chronicle of Higher Education*, April 15, 2016.

104. F: Eric Posner, "The World Doesn't Love the First Amendment," *Slate*, September 25, 2012; Steven H. Shiffrin, "The Dark Side of the First Amendment," 61 *UCLA Law Review*, 480, (2014) and *What's Wrong with the First Amendment* (Cambridge: Cambridge University Press, 2016).

105. Anne Neal, "Committing to Academic Freedom," *Baltimore Sun*, September 30, 2015.

our community to be engaged in rigorous debate, discussion and even disagreement. At times that may challenge you and even cause discomfort."[106]

Geoffrey R. Stone, former Dean of the Law School and Provost who chaired the University of Chicago's Committee on Freedom of Expression, and Will Creeley, Vice President for Legal and Public Advocacy for F.I.R.E., wrote:

> Backed by a strong commitment to freedom of expression and academic freedom, faculty could challenge one another, their students and the public to consider new possibilities, without fear of reprisal. Students would no longer face punishment for exercising their right to speak out freely about issues most important to them. Instead of learning that voicing one's opinions invites silencing, students would learn that spirited debate is a vital necessity for the advancement of knowledge. And they would be taught that the proper response to ideas they oppose is not censorship, but argument on the merits. That after all is what a university is for.[107]

This letter was a reflection of an older tradition at Chicago. Hannah Holborn Gray, eminent historian and President of the University between 1978 and 2002, once wrote:

> Education should not be intended to make people comfortable, it is meant to make them think. Universities should be expected to provide

---

106. Scott Jaschik, "U of Chicago warns incoming students not to expect safe spaces or trigger warnings," *Inside Higher Education*, August 25, 2016. For a critique of the safe spaces concept, see K.C. Johnson, "Safe Spaces and Defending the Academic Status Quo," *Academic Questions,* Spring 2017, Vol. 30, No. 1, pp.39–46. For a journalist's history of the concept of safe spaces see, Sarah Brown and Katherine Mangan, "What 'Safe Spaces' Really Look Like on College Campuses," *The Chronicle of Higher Education,* September 16. 2016. See also, Emily Deruy, "The Fine Line Between Safe Space and Segregation," *The Atlantic,* August 2016.

107. "Restoring free speech on campus," *Washington Post,* September 25, 2015. Stone has written a brief history of academic freedom, in which he noted the long history of such freedom at the University of Chicago going back at least as far as President William Rainey Harper's 1892 declaration: "When for any reason the administration of a university attempts to dislodge a professor because of his political or religious sentiments, at that moment the institution has ceased to be a university." Geoffrey R. Stone, "Free Expression in Peril," *The Chronicle of Higher Education,* September 16, 2016. B9.

the conditions within which hard thought, and therefore strong disagreement, independent judgment, and the questioning of stubborn assumptions, can flourish in an environment of the greatest freedom.[108]

By September 2018, over 50 colleges, universities and university systems had endorsed or adopted the Chicago principles.[109] What impact adopting these principles, however, will have on the actual intellectual diversity of campus discourse remains to be studied.

On September 17, 2015, the Regents of the University of California were presented with a proposed "Statement of Principles Against Intolerance."[110] While affirming freedom of speech, the statement also condemned "derogatory language reflecting stereotypes or prejudice, or inflammatory or derogatory use of culturally recognized symbols of hate, prejudice or discrimination." The Regents did not accept this proposal which would have created a definitional minefield for those wishing to speak about such controversial issues such as illegal immigration, affirmative action, same sex marriage, abortion funding or Israeli/Palestinian conflicts, among others.

While some campuses have issued general affirmations of freedom of speech, such actions may not be enough. Sometimes universities just try to manage the occasional public relations problems, that disinviting or shouting down speakers or threatening or stealing newspapers or restricting journalists creates, by pointing out the inconsistency of those actions with their academic values. Even when they make admirable generalized lofty statements about freedom of speech, however, they may not actually change the existing smothering blanket of campus conformity on controversial issues. **If a campus does not take steps actively to promote a culture of debates or forums with divergent viewpoints about policy issues and instead remains passive, the tacit messages is that such differences of opinion, especially if they are politically incorrect, are better left unexpressed.**

---

108. Quoted in the Commission on Freedom of Expression at the University of Chicago report. https://freeexpression.uchicago.edu/sites/freeexpression.ichicago.edu/files/FOECommitteeReport.pdf.

109. Joyce Lee Malcolm, *Building a Culture of Free Expression on the American College Campus*, American Council of Trustees and Alumni, April 2018, p.34.

110. Peter Schmidt, "U. of California Proposed Statement on Intolerance Is Widely Found Intolerable," *The Chronicle of Higher Education*, September 16, 2105 and Peter Schmidt, "U. of California Struggles to Draw the Line on Intolerance," *The Chronicle of Higher Education*, September 25, 2015.

It might be expected that campuses, given their rhetoric about the citizenship goals of higher education would be centers for policy debates that affect the nation's wellbeing and the individual futures of those persons who study and work there. Yet it is notable that in the various free speech controversies in recent years, the response of campus administrators was almost never "Let's have an open debate on that issue."

If the topic is carefully defined, the speakers well prepared, and the event skillfully moderated, debates can make important contributions to on-campus policy dialogues. Consequently, the research reported here about the topics, participants, and frequency of on campus debates or forums with divergent viewpoints may provide new empirical information about the state of public discourse about national public issues in American colleges and universities.

D. Debates in American Historical Context

Unfortunately, debates have gotten a bad reputation among many Americans because they don't view models of constructive debates in the media and are turned off by what appears to be merely verbal pugilistics. The problem of ugly presidential debates goes back much farther than the 2016 election. Walter Cronkite wrote in 1998 about these debates:

> Here is a means to present to the American people a rational explanation of the major issues that face the nation, and alternative explanations to their solution. Yet the candidates participate only with the guarantee of a format that defies meaningful discourse. They should be charged with sabotaging the electoral process.[111]

The kind of policy debates academic institutions should sponsor should not resemble boxing matches or even worse mixed martial arts (MMA), but instead should invite participants who regard the fully qualified person across from them as a proponent of a different set of alternatives, not an opponent to be trounced. Wherever possible debaters should begin with the premises they hold in common. For example, we agree with the concept of separation of powers or federalism, but. . . . We agree that the United

---

111. As quoted in an article overviewing thirty years of Presidential debates by Jill Lepore, "The State of Debate," *The New Yorker*, September 19, 2016.

States should have enforceable borders or that health care is both an individual and societal responsibility, but our current policies . . . . The moral, political, and economic consequences of a policy can then be explored in an atmosphere of mutual respect, while always being mindful of the unintended consequences of well-intended policies. In an academic setting a successful outcome can be (a) some audience members can better articulate the positions they previously held; (b) some change their minds or (c) some, though better informed, are still grappling with the right course of action.

Debate is not the only way to examine public policy alternatives and sometimes not the best format, but it potentially has an important role to play in contemporary politics as it has in our nation's past. Madison set out the overarching basic issue in a democracy in his classic language in The Federalist 51:

> If men were angels, no government would be necessary. If angels were to govern men, neither external nor internal controls on government would be necessary. In framing a government which is to be administered by men over men, the great difficulty lies in this: You must first enable the government to control the governed; and in the next place, oblige it to control itself. A dependence on the people is no doubt the primary control on the government; but experience has taught mankind the necessity of auxiliary precautions.[112]

Defining and balancing the "auxiliary precautions" are questions about which every generation of Americans must grapple. The great issues of federalism, separation of powers, and political representation were fiercely contested in Constitutional Convention debates.[113] In the aftermath of those debates, the Federalists and the Anti-Federalists blanketed the country with tracts for and against the new Constitution. While the Federalists won in 1788 after close contests in New York and Virginia, the Anti-Federalists were successful three years later in forcing the drafting and

---

112. Alexander Hamilton, James Madison, and John Jay, *The Federalist Papers*, ed. Jim Miller (Mineola, N.Y.: Dover Publications, 2014).

113. Catherine Drinker Bowen, *Miracle at Philadelphia* (Boston: Little, Brown and Company, 1985) and Joseph J. Ellis, *The Quartet* (New York: Alfred A. Knopf, 2015).

eventual adoption of the first ten amendments, the Constitution's Bill of Rights as "auxiliary precautions."

The issue of slavery could not be settled until decades later. In 1858, however, there was a series of seven debates in Illinois between the two-term incumbent Senator Stephen A. Douglas and an obscure Springfield lawyer who had served one term in the House of Representatives. The debates were held across that state and were also of keen interest to citizens from other states. Chicago newspapers sent stenographers to record the complete text of the debates which were then reprinted in full by newspapers across the country. Lincoln subsequently lost his bid for the Senate seat, but his logic and passion ignited the abolitionist movement and propelled him to the presidency in 1860.[114]

In the modern period, debates are still an important element of American government. Debates between candidates for the Presidency attract some of the largest audiences of any television event. Congressional committee or floor debates can open a window for public discussion of important issues. Every year, the published majority, concurring, and dissenting opinions of Supreme Court Justices record their debates on important constitutional and statutory issues, and even on the meaning of the rule of law itself. These debates attract great interest in the United States and influence international jurisprudence.

There is a long history of debating on American campuses, but recently student debating has functioned more like a sport for a select few fast-talking exhibitionists than as a vehicle for seriously engaging about policy issues for broad audiences. Ivy League universities had a tradition of student debating about public policy beginning in the nineteenth century. In 1908, Harvard, Yale and Princeton began to hold annual Triangulars focusing on economic and political policies and attracted large audiences and high-ranking officials.[115] That tradition of substantive and significant student debating for broad audiences has been almost entirely abandoned.

Currently, there are two major college debating organizations, the American Parliamentary Debate Association (ADPA) and the National

---

114. Allen C. Guelzo, *Lincoln and Douglas: The Debates that Defined America* (New York: Simon and Schuster, 2008) and Harry K Jaffa, *Crisis of a House Divided: An Interpretation of the Lincoln-Douglas Debates Fiftieth Anniversary Edition* (Chicago: University of Chicago Press, 2009).

115. "History," Harvard Speech and Parliamentary Debate Society.

Parliamentary Debate Association (NDPA). The ADPA is the older of the two, founded in 1982 and composed mostly of eastern schools,[116] while the NDPA, established in 1991 has members mostly west of the Mississippi.[117] Despite their names, these organizations rarely encourage the kinds of substantive debates that characterize governmental parliamentary debates. To the contrary, these college debates are meant to test the quick responses and wit of the debaters, not their depth of knowledge about any subject. Typically, in ADPA tournaments the resolutions to be debated are announced 15–20 minutes in advance and there is a ban on quoted evidence or even consultation of evidence that was not gathered in the short preparation time allowed. In NDPA debates, new topics are assigned every round and preparation time is also very limited. In both organizations, debaters operate within very strict time limits and are judged by officials who declare winners and award trophies. Most debates are held off campus with audiences predominantly of other debaters. In short, these debate organizations and formats follow a sort of club sport competition model which can be useful for the selected participants. They are not intended to provide in-depth analysis of any subject or to expose the general student body to important national policy alternatives.

Why focus on debates or forums where the participants have divergent views? As Harvard President Faust told a 2016 UMBC commencement, "Now, as you join the fellowship of college graduates, you have intellectual responsibilities to our society as well. You have the responsibility to model reason and reasoned debates; to value facts and insist they inform our public discourse."[118] To take up those "intellectual responsibilities," however, students need to be taught to attend, listen, and critique policy debates which are difficult lessons to learn if campuses do not sponsor such debates.

If student debate organizations now rarely take up the responsibility for bringing to campus audiences divergent views about major policy issues and, if campus leaderships would agree, at least abstractly, that such exposure would be useful for citizenship training, then faculty, politicians, lobbyists, and non-profit leaders could fulfill this role. Does fostering a culture of policy debates actually happen?

---

116. American Parliamentary Debate Association http://www.adpaweb.org/.

117. National Parliamentary Debate Association http://www.parlidebate.org/.

118. Carrie Wells, "Faust tells grads about growing education gap," *The Baltimore Sun*, May 20, 2016, p. 2.

Chapter II.
Campus Survey Research Methodology

The question for this research is whether open policy forums with speakers taking divergent positions are regularly occurring on campus and if so, what topics are discussed, and who are the participants? The sources for investigating this question are campus events calendars that list on the Internet activities available to all connected to the campus community. Generally these accessible calendars provide a comprehensive overview of policy events open to the whole campus.

About twenty percent of the campuses we wished to include had to be dropped because their website calendars were non-existent or highly incomplete in terms of listing debates, forums or lectures on public policy in 2014 and 2015. For example, at the University of California, San Diego, the Administrator of the UCSD Calendar of Events wrote our researcher, "Unfortunately, we completely revised our calendar in 2016, and the old calendar of events, was completely dumped, so we no longer have any record of those events, prior to that time."[119] In contrast, at these same institutions, it was easy to find electronically the outcomes of their athletic contests going back many years. For example, UCSD has a Softball Record book that electronically lists Tritons' sport minutia back to 1977 and has similar baseball statistics going back to 1980. Almost all campuses have

---

119. Aaron Borovey email to Adam Shulman, 5/14/2018. UC-Irvine also did not preserve it 2014–2015 calendar after changing it calendar software provider. The University of North Carolina, Chapel Hill has moved its calendar records to unc.edu which it says is not available to the public. Georgia Tech and the University of Maryland College Park did not have accessible calendars for 2014 and 2105.

persons assigned to compiling and publicizing sport's information, but similar attention is not given to preserving their records of institutional intellectual activity.

This research reports on evidence gathered from 97 campuses and 28 law schools enrolling at least 991,802 students from a stratified sample of institutions selected from the top ranked campuses in the *U.S. News and World Report* categories (top national private and public research universities, top regional private and public universities, top national liberal arts colleges, and major religiously affiliated institutions).[120] A subset of Indiana campuses was also studied to see if there were regional variations.[121] By focusing on "top" institutions, the results are skewed toward campuses with more resources. Many of the top liberal arts colleges in this sample had endowment of over a billion dollars. The lack of policy events may be much greater at lower ranked liberal arts institutions, such as those in the Indiana sample. For each sampled institution, the topic, date, campus sponsor, speakers with their affiliations was recorded for the calendar years 2014 and 2015. (See Figure A)

Some definitions are necessary to set the boundaries of this research, particularly what constitutes a policy event accessible to all members of the campus community. Such events should be open without a registration fee and be sponsored by a campus office, program or group. Rental of campus facilities for conventions, advocacy groups or political candidates are not counted. Presentations of departmental research and capstone seminars or degree defenses would not ordinarily fit this definition because those formats are rarely open to the entire campus.

There are limitations in this research as a measure of the whole climate of campus political discourse and it does not purport to be such. This research does not examine what occurs in individual classrooms or whether those lectures and readings are reasonably well balanced. Particularly, in social sciences courses many policy issues will be discussed, but only a small fraction of the student body will take classes in American history or

---

120. Not every campus that had an accessible calendar for 2014 had one for 2015 and vice versa, so these totals are for campuses that had accessible calendars for either year.

121. Most of the research on Indiana campuses was completed by Jack Simon, Hanover College Class of 2017.

the Constitution, economic policy or foreign affairs, for example.[122] This research also does not include what information campus members may find online, sources which frequently exist in an ideological echo chamber. It does not cover what faculty or students publish regarding public policy or what policy discussions may find their way into student newspapers. It does not include the topics, affiliations or viewpoints of individual speakers invited by campuses or their organizational components, in its aggregate Figures, though such information is usually recorded "below the grid" in campus data sheets when it is available. Such speeches may be valuable occasions, but frequently many in the audience will not be acquainted with the speaker's arguments before the event and will not be able instantly to evaluate them. Further, those giving the lectures usually are considered guests of the campus, receiving transportation, meals, sometimes lodging and honoraria. Challenging the guest speaker's command of the literature, methodology or understanding of unintended consequences and the wisdom of those responsible for bringing that person to the campus is awkward. To be effective it might require a sustained exchange that would probably be regarded as inappropriate by the rest of the audience. In these settings, students, in particular, may be reluctant to question the positions of the invited lecturer.

Professor of Journalism Marie K. Shanahan has articulated the framework of this research:

> Young people are unlikely to learn how to engage in civil public discourse from their social media interactions. If civility requires emotional security, then students have to practice. And college educators like me need to do a better job embracing the critical role of debate facilitator and debate moderator.
>
> Lectures by professors and campus protests rightly focus attention on important topics but both are inherently one-sided. College stu-

---

122. Citing an American Council of Trustees and Alumni study, Douglas Belkin pointed out that only 18 percent of a sample of 1,098 public and private colleges and universities required a course in American history or government and only 3 percent in economics. *Wall Street Journal*, October 15, 2014. See also, Jasper Scherer, "Most History Majors at Top US Schools Can Skip American History," *Fortune*, June 30, 2016 and Melissa Korn, "Few Top Schools Require History Majors to Broadly Study U.S.'s past," *The Wall Street Journal*, June 29, 2016.

dents also need thoughtful opportunities to participate in structured debates outside their filter bubbles, so they practice listening to and arguing dissenting points of view.[123]

In a debate or forum with divergent views, it is likely that the multiple speakers will be familiar with the other participants' positions and will have the data and skills to expose weaknesses and contradictions in them. The student audiences in such settings also are more likely to be ideologically diverse and the result less likely to be simple confirmation bias.

A debate between well-prepared participants will not only permit an audience to examine the facts and theories that underlie different policy positions, but also the unintended consequences, implementation problems, and costs and benefits of a program. It should lead the audience to expect and respect the concept that opposing policy positions are normal in a democracy. Ad homonym arguments, guilt by association aspersions, and snark attacks that treat difficult policy questions as occasions for comedy or ridicule will be more easily recognized and discredited. For students, especially, it should sharpen intelligent listening and questioning skills, thus improving classroom and single presenter lectures where policy issues are presented. Debates should also teach college students about the complexity of solving the nation's and the world's problems, while recognizing the students' immediate role as voters and their future role as leaders. Description of these events is a first step toward developing reform efforts to increase a tolerance of diverse ideas in academia.

As it turns out, on-campus policy debates, though rare, are easy to identify in events calendars. Multi-speaker forums are more common. It was sometimes difficult, however, to determine whether the participants were invited because they represented divergent viewpoints, whether the panel members were just friends of the convener, or whether the panels were structured to advocate a single perspective.

Multi-speaker campus policy forums, most often dealing with race or gender, were still classified as "uncertain viewpoint "events in this research, despite what appeared to be the common ideological backgrounds of the panelists or sponsors. At Stanford, for example, a 2014 panel on "Ferguson: America's Movement for Racial Justice" was sponsored by the African

---

123. Marie K. Shanahan, "Yes Campuses Should be Safe Spaces—for Debate," *The Chronicle of Higher Education*, February 5, 2016, p. A48.

and African American Studies Department, the Black Community Services Center, the Institute for Diversity in the Arts, Black Student Union, NAACP, ResED and Urban Studies. The panelists were a Missouri State Senator (D), a Morehouse College professor, and two "activists." In 2015, Stanford's African and African American Studies Department and Institute for Diversity in the Arts sponsored a panel "Dare to Struggle: grassroots activists on the decades long fight to end police brutality and mass incarceration." The panelists were five "activists" identified with no organizational titles and representatives from Million Hoodies Movement for Justice, Californians for Safety and Justice, and Community Justice Network for Youth. Washington University, St. Louis' Assembly Series 2014 forum on "Marriage Equality and the GOP" featured the executive director of the Log Cabin Republicans, the first openly gay Republican presidential candidate, and a "media personality gay rights activist." That University's Department of Women's, Gender, and Sexuality Studies also sponsored a 2014 forum titled "Out of the Margins: Carving Space of Trans Women of Color" with four trans-activist panelists.

Even panelists within one part of the spectrum of American policy viewpoints, there can be some differences of opinions. In that case, where possible, it was helpful to follow up with the sponsor or moderator of the panel or view the event on a website to find out whether divergent views were expressed. Not every university panel needs to represent the full spectrum of relevant policy viewpoints, but universities should ask themselves whether they are fully educating their students, if some policy perspectives are never heard on campus.

A. Research Results

Figure A displays the data sheets used to record multi-speaker policy events from campus calendars. Policy events were recorded using expansive definitions, if they fit at all the categories on the grid or in the "other" category. Figures B and C classify these events as debates or forums with probable divergent viewpoints, or forums with uncertain divergent viewpoints in six institutional categories. Again expansive definitions were used in classifying events. Figures D and E record the frequency with which various topics were treated in debates or open forums on the campuses in this research sample and also examine whether they were sponsored by a law school or not.

Figure A Open Campus Debates or Forum Project Data Sheet 2014 and 2015

Campus name: _____

Campus contact(s)

Name: _____

Position: _____ email: _____ phone: _____

UMBC Researcher: _____

Topic	Date/Event Classification	Sponsor	Speakers	Comments
1 Income inequality				
2 Environmental climate change policy				
3 Abortion policy				
4 Same sex marriage/GLBT issues				
5 Immigration, refugee policy				
6 Education financing, accountability and other issues				
7 Governmental, financing and debt				
8 Governmental regulatory procedures and policy				
9 Health care financing and other policies				

Topic	Date/Event Classification	Sponsor	Speakers	Comments
10 Constitutional government, federalism, separation of powers				
11 International trade policy				
12 U.S role Middle East and Afghanistan				
13 U.S Role Russia and China				
14 Crime and criminal justice				
15 Civil rights				
16 Civil liberties and privacy				
17 Objectionable speech policies and practices				
18 Sexual assault policies and practices				
19 Affirmative action/ diversity policies				
20 Housing and urban development				
21 Politics and Elections				
22 Gun policies				
23 Terrorism policies				
24 Other				

Figures B and C show the results by institutional categories taken from completed campus data sheets for 2014 and 2015.

Figure B On Campus Policy Debates and Forums by Institutional Categories 2014

Institutional Categories	Total Sampled Institutions (Total Enrollment)	Number of Policy Debates	Policy Debates per 1000 Students	Policy Forums With Probable Divergent viewpoints	Policy Forums With Probable Divergent Viewpoints per 1000 Students	Number of Policy Forums with Uncertain Viewpoints	Policy Forums Uncertain Viewpoint per 1000 Students
Top National Private and Public Universities	20 (383,676)	36	.09	74	.19	108	.28
Top Regional Private Universities	11 (71,262)	4	.056	5	.072	18	.253
Top Regional Public Universities	9 (183,679)	5	.027	1	.005	12	.066
Top Liberal Arts	15 (29,118)	12	.413	23	.793	40	1.38
Indiana Campuses*	13 (81,334)	2	.025	0	.00	3	.037
Religiously affiliated Institutions	21 (242,733)	8	.033	25	.103	25	.103
	92 991,802	67	.067	123	.124	206	.207

Top Private Universities included Brown, Cal Tech, Chicago, Columbia, Dartmouth, Georgetown, Harvard, Johns Hopkins, MIT, Northwestern, Notre Dame, Pennsylvania, Princeton, Rice, Stanford, Vanderbilt, and Wake Forest. Yale and Boston College did not have accessible master calendars.
Top Public Universities included Michigan, UC Los Angeles, and U.C Berkeley. A number of top public universities did not preserve their calendars in any searchable electronic form. See footnote 119.

* These campuses are mostly liberal arts colleges with the exception of Ball State University (enrollment 20,000) and Purdue University (enrollment 40,451). Notre Dame University in South Bend Indiana is classified in the top national private category, though it could also be categorized as a religiously affiliated institution.

Figure C On Campus Policy Debates and Forums by Institutional Categories 2015

Institutional Categories	Total Institutions (Total Enrollment)	Number of Policy Debates	Policy Debates per 1000 Students	Policy Forums With Probable Divergent Viewpoints	Policy Forums With Probable Divergent Viewpoints per 1000 Students	Number of Policy Forums with Uncertain Viewpoints	Policy Forums Uncertain Viewpoint per 1000 Students
Top National Private and Public Universities	20 (383,679)	48	.125	95	.248	163	.425
Top Regional Private Universities	16 (91,304)	3	.032	7	.077	15	.165
Top Regional Public Universities	8 (147,605)	1	.007	3	.02	8	.054
Top Liberal Arts	16 (31,031)	5	.161	9	.29	37	1.19
Indiana Campuses*	13 (81,334)	0	.00	23	.037	0	.00
Religiously affiliated Institutions	23 (232,126)	12	.053	43	.19	34	.146
	95 929,829	69	.074	160	.172	257	.309

See classifications of campuses in Figure B.

Figure D Policy Topics and Number of Debates or Probable Divergent Viewpoint Forums in National Top Campuses in 2014 and 2015 (data from 20 campuses and 12 law schools)

Topic	Policy Debates Non-Law School Sponsored	Policy Debates Law School Sponsored	Divergent Viewpoint Forums Non-Law School Sponsored	Divergent Viewpoint Forums Law School Sponsored
1. Income inequality	6	0	7	2
2. Environmental climate change policy	16	1	3	0
3. Abortion policy	0	0	0	2
4. Same sex marriage/ GLBT issues	1	1	0	3
5. Immigration, refugee policy	1	0	1	0
6. Education financing, accountability and other issues	11	0	11	1
7. Governmental, financing and debt	0	0	0	1
8. Governmental regulatory procedures and policy	2	1	1	6
9. Health care financing and other policies	19	1	6	2
10. Constitutional government, federalism, separation of powers	2	11	2	16

Topic	Policy Debates Non- Law School Sponsored	Policy Debates Law School Sponsored	Divergent Viewpoint Forums Non- Law School Sponsored	Divergent Viewpoint Forums Law School Sponsored
11. International trade policy	0	0	0	0
12. U.S role Middle East and Afghanistan	11	2	6	1
13. U.S role Russia and China	7	0	2	1
14. Crime and criminal justice	7	3	8	5
15. Civil rights	3	0	6	5
16. Civil liberties and privacy	4	1	4	6
17. Objectionable speech policies and practices	2	0	0	0
18. Sexual assault policies and practices	0	0	0	0
19. Affirmative action/ diversity policies	3	1	0	1
20 Housing and urban develop- ment	1	0	0	0
21. Politics and elections	10	0	9	0
22. Gun policies	1	0	0	2
23. Terrorism policies	7	1	1	2
24. Other	3	1	4	0

Figure F Policy Topics and Number of Debates or Probable Divergent Viewpoint Forums in Non-National Top Campuses in 2014 and 2015 (data from 77 campuses and 16 law schools)

Topic	Policy Debates Non-Law School Sponsored	Policy Debates Law School Sponsored	Policy Divergent Viewpoint Forums Non-Law School Sponsored	Policy Divergent Viewpoint Forums Law School Sponsored
1. Income inequality	0	0	1	0
2. Environmental climate change policy	2	0	8	0
3. Abortion policy	0	0	0	0
4. Same sex marriage/ GLBT issues	3	1	0	0
5. Immigration, refugee policy	0	0	0	0
6. Education financing, accountability and other issues	1	0	2	2
7. Governmental financing and debt	1	0	0	0
8. Governmental regulatory procedures and policy	1	0	0	0
9. Health care financing and other policies	0	1	0	2
10. Constitutional government, federalism, separation of powers	0	0	0	1
11. International trade policy	0	0	0	0
12. U.S role Middle East and Afghanistan	1	0	3	1
13. U.S role Russia and China	0	0	1	0

Topic	Policy Debates Non-Law School Sponsored	Policy Debates Law School Sponsored	Policy Divergent Viewpoint Forums Non-Law School Sponsored	Policy Divergent Viewpoint Forums Law School Sponsored
14. Crime and criminal justice	1	2	1	10
15 Civil rights	0	0	0	0
16. Civil liberties and privacy	1	0	0	1
17. Objectionable speech policies and practices	0	0	0	3
18. Sexual assault policies and practices	0	0	0	0
19. Affirmative action/ diversity policies	1	0	1	0
20. Housing and urban development	0	0	0	0
21. Politics and elections	3	0	6	5
22. Gun policies	1	0	1	0
23. Terrorism policies	0	0	2	2
24. Other	0	0	5	5

B. Empirical Conclusions

It might be expected that institutions of higher education which are heavily publicly funded, whether they are managed by state or private trustees, would believe it a priority to expose students to policy issue debates to give them the ability to exercise their franchise intelligently. As Figures B and C shows, some issues debated everywhere else in society are rarely debated at all on these campuses. Environmental and health policy were frequent topics, while immigration, abortion, government financing, international trade, speech, sexual assault, affirmative action, and even gun policies were almost never debated publicly on campus in 2104 and 2015. No wonder, so many in higher education were surprised at the outcome of the 2016 election. The issues that motivated so many voters were not much discussed where these educators and students lived and worked.

For most students in American higher education, the opportunity to hear on-campus debates about important public policy issues does not exist. Free speech for controversial speakers dominates the press coverage, but the important story of the absence of policy debates is missed. This research shows a very uneven pattern in the availability of policy debates or forums with probable divergent viewpoints. The data generally show a paucity of policy debates for most students. Excluding the top private and public national universities, there were 20 policy debates and 63 forums with probable divergent viewpoints on 76 different campuses surveyed enrolling about 440,000 students over the two year 2014–2015 period examined. That is about one such event per campus per year. By comparison, there were 48 policy debates and 95 policy forums with probable divergent viewpoints on the top 20 national universities, enrolling 383,679 students. Within these two overarching categories, there was a wide variety in campus sponsorship of topics and frequencies.

There are two exceptions to this pattern. Very well-endowed large institutions with a variety of institutes and centers host many policy forums. The 20 top national private and public universities in our sample each have endowments considerably exceeding $1 billion dollars. Frequently, think tanks and research centers are appendages to elite institutions, but do not offer regular classes. Therefore, they must sponsor forums, seminars, and workshops to raise the private funding they need to remain viable, though these events are not often geared to undergraduates.[124] For example, Harvard with its $38 billion endowment hosted 117 debates and forums (though not all with divergent viewpoints) in 2014 and 2015, while it's nearby neighbor the University of Massachusetts, Boston with its $79 million endowment sponsored 4 such events. The very well-endowed research institutions are disproportionately located on coastal states, but there does

---

124. Some campus debates feature such notable speakers that tickets might be required. For example, Noam Chomsky and Alan Dershowitz debated "Israel and Palestine after Disengagement," at Harvard, January 28, 2011. Stanford hosted a debate on energy policy between two Noble Prize winners, Steven Chu and Burton Richter, (pro) and Ralph Cavanagh and Daniel Kammen, co-directors of NRDC's energy program (con). (Stanford Precourt Energy Efficiency Center News. June 9, 2016). However, such star power is not necessary to provide students with model substantive debates.

not seem to be a regional difference in the overall pattern. In Indiana, Notre Dame University, with its $8.4 billion endowment, hosted a variety of debates and forums with divergent views, while 10 Hoosier liberal arts colleges, as well as Purdue and Ball State University, sponsored few or none.

The other exception is law schools which believe that debates or forums with divergent viewpoints are a useful preparation for a profession that frequently involves adversarial presentations. The Federalist Society (right-oriented) and the American Constitutional Society (left-oriented) frequently host debates and forums on both general legal policy questions and on more narrow court case interpretations.[125] Both the Yale and Stanford law schools recently held all day seminars, sponsored by their student chapters of The Federalist Society, featuring many prominent professors on the subject of intellectual diversity. The Stanford program's premise was:

> Universities have traditionally provided a forum for the free exchange of ideas between and among faculty and student. But how robust can discourse be when most everyone shares the same thoughts and opinions. How can a professor tackle a controversial research topic or a student express an unpopular opinion, if he or she is terrified of finding or saying the "wrong" thing?[126]

Although undergraduates are generally welcome to attend policy events at campus law schools or research institutes, it is doubtful many do. About half of the nation's 200 or so law schools are located some distance from the undergraduate campus. Even, as in the case of The Federalist Society which is committed to including more undergraduates in the audience for its sponsored law school debates, it has proved a tough sell.[127]

While a disproportionate number of campus debates are held in law schools, even these forums are not immune from those who would seek to silence speakers or ideas they do not like. In the fall of 2017, a debate featuring both liberal and conservative viewpoints on immigration policy was scheduled at the Seattle University Law School as a part of Social Justice

---

125. The law school Federalist events are more likely to be debates, while the ACS events are more likely to be multi-speaker forums advocating policies.

126. http://w.w.w.fed-soc-org/events/details/stanford-intellctual-diversity-com.

127. Interview with Eugene Meyer, President, Lee Liberman Otis, Senior Vice President, and Peter Redpath, Vice President and Director Student Division. July 19, 2016.

Monday to be co-hosted by the School's Access to Justice Institute and the student chapter of The Federalist Society. After a student protest over the School's sponsorship of the debate, the timing of the debate, and really the debate itself, Dean Annette Clark withdrew School sponsorship in an email to students arguing that the Trump administration had:

> generated great fear within vulnerable immigrant communities and has caused real harm, making discussions of immigration policy that include a conservative viewpoint even more painful and anxiety-and anger-producing for those individuals and families who are at risk (and for their allies).[128]

The following spring, students at the Lewis & Clark Law School shouted down Christina Hoff Sommers, who is critical of some types of feminism and had been invited by the local Federalist Society chapter.[129] Protestors attempted to block the door to the room where she had been scheduled to speak, though the College circumvented them by bringing Sommers in through a back entrance. But her ordeal was not over. Once inside she was confronted with student protestors who interrupted portions of her speech and, at the request of the Law School's Dean of Diversity and Inclusion Janet Stevenson, Sommers had to cut short her remarks. The protesting students sang "Which side are you on friends? Which side are you on? No platform for fascists, no platform at all. We will fight for justice until Christina's gone." Dean Stevenson conceded that the law students blocking the lecture hall entrance and interrupting the speech violated college rules. She also noted that there were many grounds to criticize Sommers, but that it was inappropriate to call her a "fascist." The Dean said, "In the law school it is important to define the terms you are using and to apply the facts to support the allegations you have made." Actually hearing out a speaker and raising issues in Q &A might help law students with making those distinctions, but the Dean was not willing to state what penalties might be invoked for those violating the Law School's rules.

---

128. "Seattle Law Dean Apologizes For Scheduling a DACA Debate Featuring Conservative Viewpoints," http://johnathanturley.org/2017/10/11/ seattle-law-dean-apologizes... See also Cal Thomas. "Censorship in Seattle," *The San Diego Union- Tribune,* October 1, 2017.

129. Scott Jaschik, "Students interrupt several portions of speech by Christina Hoff Sommers," *Inside Higher Education.* March 6, 2018.

A month later, students at the City University of New York Law School heckled and shouted down another Federalist Society speaker Professor Josh Blackwood of the South Texas College of Law disrupting the first ten minutes of his address.[130] Many students scattered around the lecture hall interrupted him as he attempted to talk about the dimensions of free speech. From their perspective, CUNY should not have permitted Blackwood to speak because the law school had a mission focused on "the public interest, public service and diversifying the legal profession." Some students said the law school was giving a platform for the idea that other speakers—whose presence causes pain to some students—should be allowed to appear on campus. At least one student held up a sign for the camera which read, "Federalist Society was founded to uphold white supremacy." Law School Dean Mary Lu Bilek supported the protestors because they were non-violent, did not violate any University policy, and, after making their points, left the room. She pointed out that "CUNY Law students are encouraged to develop their own perspectives on the law in order to be prepared to confront the most difficult legal and social issues as lawyers promoting the values of fairness, justice and equality." Apparently, for some students, "no platforming" is consistent with developing personal perspectives on difficult issues.

Overall, higher education has struggled to create policies to respond to the "Heckler's Veto" which the Supreme Court dealt with in its 1949 *Terminiello v. Chicago* decision holding that governments must protect speech, even when might provoke an audience "to disturb the peace."[131] Crafting a policy that permits protesting a speaker outside the room reserved for the speech without blocking the entrance or otherwise disrupting the rights of those who wish to hear the speaker should not be too difficult.

Perhaps a majority of campus multi-speaker forums are sponsored by campus advocacy groups (environmental, racial and ethnic, women, and LGBTQ) and are focused on building support for their causes. Some examples of purposely exposing undergraduates to diverse policy views, however, were discovered in this research and there are doubtless more. Among

130. Scott Jaschik, "Guest lecture on free speech at CUNY law school heckled," *Inside Higher Education*, April 16, 2018. For the view of the NAS CUNY Association of Scholars on the details of this incident and criticism of the Dean's response, see their letter to CUNY Milliken http://nas,org/articles/cunys_lawless_law_students.

131. 337 U.S.1, 4.

top liberal arts colleges, which have had more than their share of disrupted speech,[132] the Goldfarb Center for Public Affairs and Civic Engagement (Colby), the Center for Freedom and Western Civilization (Colgate), and the Center for the Study of American Democracy (Kenyon) offer robust public policy programing.

At Brown University, the Janus Institute's mission is to "increase viewpoint diversity in the academy, with a special focus on the social sciences" and it has been successful in inviting several speakers with divergent viewpoints to the campus. But sometimes these events at Brown have been disrupted by students who wanted speech suppressed. The history of these incidents has been captured in a chilling thirteen minute documentary.[133] Perhaps there is some change in store. An undergraduate sophomore, Greer Brigham, "longtime Democrat and Hilary Clinton campaign volunteer," like many others was shocked at the outcome of the 2016 election. Feeling a bit blindsided, he, with a small group of other students, examined the backgrounds of speakers invited to Brown in 2017. They found that 95% were "liberals".[134] So they created an organization called SPEAK to invite speakers to campus with more diverse backgrounds. *The Chronicle of Higher Education* SPEAK story is titled, "Conservative Voices Welcome at Brown" and the accompanying picture shows University President Christina Parson moderating a discussion with Jeb Bush.[135] SPEAK makes it clear that they will not invites "fringe" speakers, such as Ann Coulter, but it is also not certain whether they are inviting speakers from the Administration

132. Richard Reeves and Dimitrios Halikias, "Illiberal Arts Colleges: Pay More, Get Less (free speech)." Brookings Institution, March 14, 2017.

133. John Tomasi, "Free Inquiry v. Social Justice at Brown University," *The Heterodox Academy*. website, July 21, 2016. See also Scott Jaschik, "Free Speech at Brown (Again)," *Inside Higher Education,* November 7, 2013.

134. This remarkable ten page document is titled "Brown University Speakers Report: Monitoring Our School's Commitment to Diversity of Thought 2017." It examined the partisan identification and campaign contributions of 223 Brown political lecturers in 2017 and found only a tiny fraction did not match the party identifications of Brown faculty and students. Thus the problem of confirmation bias is high. The Brown administration responded that the SPEAK study "… implies that a scholar, researcher, academic, injected their personal views into their scholarship which contributes to an erosion in public confidence. It suggests that facts are malleable expressions of belief. That's where our country is going right now, that facts are malleable—we just don't think that is true."

135. Jenny Bauer-Wolf, May 4, 2018. Jeb Bush won only three delegates (New Hampshire) and withdrew early from the 2016 Republican nomination race, so it not quite clear why anyone thought he was the exemplar of "Conservative Voices."

that actually won the 2016 election or are sponsoring debates where more controversy might be aired than when a campus president moderates the discussion.

Another student-initiated attempt to create dialogue on political and cultural issues is Bridges USA. Roge Karma, Notre Dame University '18 began it on his campus and it has grown to sponsor small scale events for students across the country. He envisions the organization as something that could grow into a "grass roots movement and help unite the country through respectful discourse and open-mindedness."[136]

A similar faculty effort to promote discourse across partisan divisions is the Better Angels project created by David Blankenhorn after the 2016 election. Named after a phrase used by President Lincoln in his First Inaugural Address in 1861. Better Angels based in New York works at community level dialogue, but also at promoting the concept of parliamentary debates on several campuses.[137]

The James Madison Program for American Institutions and Ideals at Princeton University, led by Professor Robert George, has a record of bringing a variety of speakers, some controversial, to campus without causing disruption.[138] The topics range from political philosophy to more applied issues. Most of the events are lectures with some round table added, but there are not many actual debates. For example, on October 3, 2017, the program sponsored an event titled "Fighting Campus Rape and Respecting Due Process" which might have occasioned a debate, but the two speakers were K.C. Johnson and Stuart Taylor Jr, who had co-authored an insightful book on that subject.[139]

A similarly named university institution is the James Madison Center for Civic Engagement at James Madison University, founded in 2017, which states its purpose as advancing the legacy of James Madison by preparing individuals to be active and responsible citizens.[140] Its early pro-

---

136. Tara Nieuwesteeg, "Across the Great Divide." *Notre Dame Magazine*, Summer, 2018, pp.5–8.

137. ACTA, "Better Angels Counters Polarization on Campus," Vol. XXIII, No.4, 2017–2018.

138. https//jmp.princeton.edu/events/past. https;//www.better-angels.org.

139. *The Campus Rape Frenzy: The Attack on Due Process at America's Universities* (New York: Encounter Books, 2017).

140. Margaret M. Mulrooney, "Campus Spotlight: Liberty and Learning at JMU," Forbes Brand Voice, August 10, 2017.

gramming seems clearly to have a service/engagement focus rather than the intellectual debate side of citizen preparation, although initial programs featured three days of "poverty simulation," a dialogue on "Heritage vs Hate-Symbols of the South" and "Toxic Masculinity." Speakers were not listed, but the invitation was for "students to come together to engage in dialogue about a topic in diversity and social justice."[141]

The Institute for Humane Studies sponsors and funds debates and public policy lectures at a number of campuses. At Northwood University (MI), debates have been held on marriage equality, minimum wage, and immigration policy with a substantial number of in-person attendees and on-line participants.[142]

Strikingly, few policy on-campus debates or forums with divergent viewpoints are sponsored by political science, public administration or public policy departments. Political Science departments are much more likely to sponsor Mock Trial competitions[143] and the Model United Nations,[144] which are quite useful activities, but which take place off-campus and involve only a handful of select students. For the vast majority of undergraduates at liberal arts colleges or regional public or private institutions without law schools or policy research institutes, there are very few campus opportunities to hear policy debates or forums with divergent viewpoints.

These findings are consistent with those of other writers who have not studied actual campus calendars. Andrea Leskes, a former executive of the Association of American Colleges and Universities, has written a "Plea for Civil Discourse: Needed, the Academy's Leadership" which linked public dissatisfaction with the state of American politics with the failure of higher education to teach the skills and appreciation for civil discourse. She defined that term as:

> (1) undertaking a serious exchange of views; (2) focusing on the issues rather than the individual espousing them; (3) defending their interpretations using verified information; (4) thoughtfully listening to what others say; (5) seeking sources of disagreement and points of

---

141. https//ems.jmu.edu/MasterCalendar/EventDetails.

142. https://iths.org/funding/faculty/partnership/dr-glenn-moots.

143. National Mock Trial Association, http://w.w.w.collegemocktrial.org.

144. National Model United Nations. This organization now almost 50 years old in 2016 had chapters on 440 colleges who come together on off-campus sites to discuss international issues.nmun.org.

common purpose; (6) embodying open-mindedness and a willingness to change minds; (7) assuming they will need to compromise and are willing to do so; (8) treating the ideas of others with respect; and (9) avoiding violence whether physical, emotional or verbal.[145]

Leskes quoted Susan Herbst that creating a culture of argument, and "the thick skin that goes along with it, are long term projects that serve democracy well."[146] And she added "One should not expect civil discourse to create a feeling of comfort; discord causes uneasiness, and a challenge to deeply held beliefs."[147] She urged that students need to be taught civil discourse techniques such as active listening, debating techniques, public speaking, and persuasive writing.[148] Leskes concluded, however, that "examples of civil discourse in general education or taught coherently across the curriculum, across the institution, or across a state system are difficult to find."[149]

In their book, *Closed Minds? Politics and Ideology in American Universities;* Jeremy Mayers, Bruce L.R. Smith, and A. Lee Fritschler reached a similar conclusion:

> Yet this ideological peace has been obtained at a high price. American universities are rarely hospitable to lively discussions of issues of public importance. They largely shun serious political debate, all but ignore what used to be called civics, and take little interest in educating students to be effective citizens.[150]

At the same time many campuses have withdrawn from sponsoring policy debates or forums with diverse intellectual viewpoints, the American public has become more politically polarized and that is reflected in those elected to represent them. A 2014 Pew Research Center survey of 10,000 adults shows that partisan divides have grown in the last twenty years.[151] By

---

145. *Liberal Education*, Fall, 2013, Vol. 99, No.4, pp. 4–5.

146. Susan. Herbst, *Rude Democracy: Civility and Incivility in American Politics* (Philadelphia: Temple University Press 2010), p.148.

147. Leskes, p.5.

148. Ibid. p.8.

149. Ibid. p.9.

150. (Washington, D.C. The Brookings Institution, 2008), text from inside book jacket.

151. Pew Research Center, "Political Polarization in the American Public," June 12, 2014.

2014, 27% of Democrats saw the Republican Party as a threat to the nation's well-being and 36% of Republicans saw Democrats as similar threat. It is likely that after the 2016 election those numbers increased on both sides. The smallest percentage of Americans who vote or contribute to campaigns are those whose ideologies combines liberal and conservative ideas. While partisan identifications overlap substantially with whether people think of themselves as liberal or conservative, the same intolerance for persons with opposing political ideas exists as for partisan identifications.[152]

We cannot and should not avoid intellectual conflict, if democracy is to flourish and progress is to be made. Particularly now, but also permanently, what is the responsibility of campuses to fund, organize, and promote policy debates by informed rational participants in civil formats? As a Catholic political philosopher, Alasdair Macintyre, has articulated:

The University (is) a place of constrained disagreement, of imposed participation in conflict, in which the central responsibility of higher education would be to initiate students into conflict. . . . Universities are places where conceptions of and standards of rational justification are elaborated, put to work in the detailed practices of enquiry, and themselves rationally evaluated, so that only from the university can the wider society learn how to conduct it is own debates, practical or theoretical, in a rational defensible way.[153]

Why aren't such debates occurring as a regular part of college education?

C. Normative Conclusions

What does this general avoidance of serious on-campus policy debates for students say about higher education's wariness about provoking controversy and its other priorities? Is there a correlation between the public's current general distain for political institutions and the news media that is supposed to cover public affairs and the fact that our best educated citizens

---

152. Matthew Hudson, "Why Liberals Aren't as Tolerant as They Think," *Politico*, May 9, 2017. This article was primarily based on research by Mark Brandt, published in *Social Psychological and Personality Science*.

153. As quoted by Eboo Patel, "Religion, Politics and the University," *Inside Higher Education*, January 28, 2018.

have been so little exposed to serious policy debates in their college years? **If we expect and need politicians to move beyond sound bites in their discussion of complex problems, higher education should provide them with discerning audiences.**

The value of exposing students to policy debates is not a right or left wing cause. In 2004, Political Research Associates (PRA), an organization that describes itself as "an independent, nonprofit research center that exposes and challenges the Right and larger oppressive movements, institutions, and forces" by doing "applied research to inform and support progressive activism that promotes equality and justice," published the results of its survey of campus activism.[154]

The report concluded:

> Contrary to popular opinion, most college students do not enjoy debating political topics. . . . Both politically uninvolved students and current student activists report they do not value political debate. Either they report they were intimidated by what they described as confrontational situations, or they did not expect engagement in formal or informal debate to affect opinions. Most student leaders in this study, with the exception of law students, believe that debate wasted their time.
>
> Many implications emerge for civil society of a generation of young people who do not value debate or who do not have the skills to engage successfully in it. We suggest that, without a politically engaged population of young people and leaders who can and will conduct conversations across differences, we cannot expect a similarly engaged population of adults.
>
> Because democracy depends on the free flow of ideas, it is endangered when there is too little respect for competing ideas or too great an imbalance of power. Such instances both diminish opportunities for sharpening critical thinking skills and silence voices. As a result fewer people openly participate in dialogues and develop and/or maintain trust in democratic institutions.

---

154. Pam Chamberlin, "Deliberate Differences: Progressive and Conservative Activism in the United States Campuses." Political Research Association, 2012. p. l.

How issues are examined and debated is a barometer of the political health of the campus and by extension the country.[155]

PRA supports "progressive activism," but most conservatives would agree with its concerns about the free flow of ideas and the health of democracy. What better way to teach critical thinking than by learning to analyze the arguments in well-reasoned debates.

Further, academic freedom overall may be invigorated by policy debates. If a campus has fostered a culture of policy debates, it is plausible that students may not be so quick to take offense at ideas that displease them. The best inoculation for unwelcome controversies over free speech may be exposing students to a culture of debate. Disrupted speeches or disinvited speakers will seem less appropriate when students have become more accustomed to lively debate. Controversies over trigger warnings, microagressions, cultural misappropriations, and "insensitive" or "problematic" phrases, may be less frequent, when campuses learn by observation to distinguish how informed people can civilly disagree.[156] "He said, she said" investigations instigated by those offended by speech may be less necessary, if the campus response was more often "Ok let's debate that issue."

Harvard's President Drew Gilpin has written:

Universities are meant to be producers not just of knowledge but also of (often inconvenient) doubt. They are creative and unruly places, home to a polyphony of voices. But at this moment in our history, universities might well ask if they have done enough to raise the deep and unsettling questions necessary to any society.... Have universities become too captive to the immediate and worldly purposes they serve?

---

155. (page number not in report).

156. Robin Wilson, "Students' Requests for Trigger Warning Grow More Varied," *The Chronicle for Higher Education*, September 18, 2015; Mason Stokes, "Don't Tell Me What is Best for My Students," *The Chronicle for Higher Education*, September 28, 2015: Scott A. Bass and Mary L. Clark, "The Gravest Threat to Colleges Comes From Within," *The Chronicle for Higher Education*, September 28, 2015; Peter Schmidt, "A Faculty's Stand on Trigger Warnings Stirs Fears Among Students," *The Chronicle for Higher Education*, October 6, 2015, September 28, 2015; Sarah Brown, "Should a Syllabus Ever Tell Students What Not to Say?" *The Chronicle for Higher Education*, October 8, 2015. For multiple perspective on trigger warnings see Emily J. M. Knox (ed.). *Trigger Warnings: History, Theory and Context* (Lanham, MD: Rowman & Littlefield, 2017).

Has the market model become the fundamental and defining identity of higher education?[157]

If a culture of vigorous public policy debates does not exist on most campuses, why is that the case? The answers must be tentative because that subject was not directly researched in this largely descriptive project. The relevant theories, however, can be divided into five categories: (1) corporatizing of higher education, (2) administrative assignments, (3) campus cultures, (4) faculty incentives, and (5) professorial ideologies. These five characteristics are deeply rooted in American higher education. They will not be easy to change, but if academic policies are just aimed at avoiding overt suppression of speech, a culture of active rational policy debate will not flourish.

(1) Higher education management has become an ever more difficult activity. The constant need to raise money, implement government regulations,[158] accommodate student consumers and other on or off campus stakeholders requires an enormous variety of talents and constant energy. To respond to these demands, universities have adopted a more corporate structure that views the older deliberative traditions of shared governance as a hindrance to seizing entrepreneurial opportunities.[159] Corporations rarely sponsor debates about public policy for their employees or customers and are not congenial environments for displays of internal divergent viewpoints about corporate policy either.[160] So as universities have become

---

157. Drew Gilpin Faust, "The University's Crisis of Purpose," *The New York Times Book Review,* September 6, 2009.

158. For a comprehensive critique of the expanded federal regulation of higher education, see U.S. Senate, Health, Education and Labor Committee, "Recalibrating Regulation of Colleges and Universities," http:/www.help.senate.gov/imo/media/Regulations_Task_Force_Report_2015_FINAL.pdf. For an analysis of the regulatory impact of Title IX alone see American Association of University Professors, *The History, Uses, and Abuses of Title IX* (Washington, D.C.: AAUP, 2016) and Robert Carle, "The Strange Career of Title IX," *Academic Questions,* Winter 2016, Vol. 29, No.4, pp. 443–453.

159. See Derek Bok, *Universities in the Marketplace: The Commercialization of Higher Education* (Princeton: Princeton University Press, 2003); Jennifer Washburn, *University, Inc.: The Corporate Corruption of Higher Education* (New York: Basic Books, 2005) and Ellen Schrecker, *The Lost Soul of Higher Education: Corporatization, the Assault on Academic Freedom and the End of the American University* (New York: The New Press, 2010).

160. Patrick Lencioni, a corporate consultant, has discovered: "And the higher up you go in the management chain, the more you find you find people spending incredible amounts

more corporate like, they have become more risk adverse and less willing to host controversial persons or ideas.[161] Almost all presidents recognize which student organizations can be mobilized to create campus disturbances about their causes or status. After all, they often successfully gain representation in the hiring process and are funded by the university. Since they will bite the hand that feeds them, better to avoid issues that would trigger their mobilization. Today, the corporate university measures and reports on multiple bottom lines, but the amount of civic literacy its students have been exposed to or gained during their studies is not on these lists.

(2) Universities have also responded to these new internal and external demands by adding layers of administrative staff.[162] It is common to have a variety of assistant provosts and deans as well as directors of athletics, residential life, student affairs, campus safety, buildings and grounds, sustainability, diversity, Title IX, etc. On the other hand, almost no higher education institution has created any administrative office responsible for seeing that a rich menu of public policy debates and forums is offered to the whole campus. As one campus professor, who does some policy programming acknowledged, when this issue was raised, "There is an administrative infra-structure vacuum here which needs to be addressed."[163]

Where campuses do emphasize citizenship responsibilities, it is frequently through service projects to the disadvantaged, disabled, underprivileged or underrepresented.[164] While certainly commendable, service by itself often does not lead to a broader understanding of the political, economic or social context in which these problems exist.

---

of time and energy to avoid the kind of passionate debates that are essential to any great team." *The Five Dysfunctions of a Team* (San Francisco: Jossey Bass, 2002).

161. The necessity to shield campus customers has been internalized by some students as well. After a faculty committee at Johns Hopkins University recommended that first semester freshmen student grades be no longer omitted from student transcripts or grade point averages, two dozen student groups protested. Erica Taicz, a protest organizer, argued. "I'm paying to have a support network academically and mentally. I can't be expected to do well in class if I'm depressed and have anxiety. If the school is worsening my anxiety, that is their problem and they need to be held accountable for that." Carrie Wells, "Changes in JHU grades policy," *The Baltimore Sun,* May 30, 2016.

162. Benjamin Ginsberg, *The Fall of the Faculty: The Rise of the All-Administrative University and Why it Matters* (New York: Oxford University Press, 2011).

163. Email to the author, March, 2017.

164. Jake New, "Colleges placing increasing importance on programs promoting civic engagement," *Inside Higher Education,* May 10, 2016.

Like faculty, these student affairs officials often have strong partisan and ideological convictions.[165] In a recent nationally representative survey of 900 "student-facing" college administrators, Samuel Abrams found those identified as liberal or very liberal outnumbered those identifying as conservative by 12 to 1. These administrators working in dorms, scheduling celebrations or entertainment, and defining what kinds of speech are permissible may have more influence, with less accountability, on campus culture than faculty.

Student affairs officials have moved into the policy discourse vacuum at many institutions and their charge is often to keep the campus calm, safe, and fun. Creating a culture of debate is not necessarily consistent with those goals and the predominant ideologies of student affairs official are not politically neutral.[166] Steven Kolowich has written: "Their duty to support the individual needs of students has often cast them as advocates of diversity and stewards of the various multicultural, women's and LGBT centers that come with it." Sometimes that has led them to prioritize the perspective of "marginalized" students when speech and debate might affect the emotional well-being or sense of inclusion.[167] Academic freedom and diversity/inclusion principles can be quite compatible, if diversity includes intellectual diversity and inclusion includes people with minority

---

165. Samuel Abrams, "Think Professors Are Liberal? Try College Administrators," *New York Times*, October 16, 2018. After Professor Abrams wrote this op-ed, there was considerable push back on campus, including some vandalizing of his office door. For Prof. Abrams' perspective on how his institution and its students responded to this incident see Robby Soave, "Sarah Lawrence Professor's Office Door Vandalized After He Criticized Leftist Bias," *Reason*, November 2, 2018. See also Madeleine Kerns, "Viewpoint Diversity Dies at Sarah Lawrence College," *National Review*, November 6, 2018.

166. For an argument that there is a deliberate effort by some student affairs bureaucracies to replace the traditional study of civics in universities with a co-curriculum of civic engagement activities that often serves ideological purposes, see David Randall, *Making Citizens: How American Universities Teach Civics* (New York: National Association of Scholars, 2017). A symposium on this controversy was published in *Academic Questions*, Summer 2017, Vol. 30, No.2, pp, 134–164. For a defense of using students in civic work projects in these politically polarized times, see Harry C. Boyte's essay in this symposium. While service projects have several useful dimensions, students who do not understand the governmental structures or the main policy issues that affect our nations cannot be fully empowered citizens. It is not an either/or question.

167. Steven Kolowich, "When Does a Student-Affairs Official Cross the Line?" *The Chronicle of Higher Education*, August 5, 2016. A26. For description of the role student affairs officers in controlling campus speech and disciplining offenders, see Richard Bernstein, *The Dictatorship of Virtue* (New York: Alfred A. Knopf, 1994).

opinions. Too often, however, the diversity/inclusion mission functions to stifle debate about controversial issues, lest some campus constituency be offended.

This perspective often leads to contentions that speech even in a lecture hall by a campus visitor with completely voluntary attendance who is not referencing any private individual makes some students feel physically threatened or "unsafe." This seems to be a new argument, not often heard in the periods of contentious civil rights or anti-war speeches in earlier periods. Where does it come from? One answer may be frequent exposure to the Internet and social media.[168] According to a 2014 Pew Research Center survey, 70% of the 18-to-24 year olds who use the Internet had experienced harassment and 26% of the women that age said they had been stalked. Many of the ugly messages attack the recipient's personal identities behind the cloak of troll anonymity.

Campuses report an increase in students who need mental health services.[169] These student attitudes and health data may contribute to the risk adverse perspectives many campus administrators hold about sponsoring campus events. Exposing students to policy debates may increase anxieties for some.

Campus cultures seek to foster respect and tolerance for those forms of officially recognized diversity based identities, which often is abstractly a good thing, but which can translate for students into an ethos of non-judgmentalism "You're Ok, I'm Ok, whatever." When Joseph DiPietro, President of the University of Tennessee (UT) system was asked by legislators whether the $5.5 million spent on "diversity" was enough, he responded that, if the day came when UT would be guaranteed there would never be a "hostile issue" about sex, religion, or political views, then the amount would be enough. He conceded that was a utopian goal, but he also failed to make the distinction between hostile behavior and divergent viewpoints.[170]

---

168. Joel Stein, "Tyranny of the Mob: Why we're losing the Internet to the culture of hate." *Time*, August 29, 2016.

169. Robin Wilson, "An Epidemic of Anguish," *The Chronicle for Higher Education*, September 4, 2015. See also, Susanna Schrobsdorff, "Anxiety, Depression and the American Adolescent," *Time* cover story, November 7, 2016.

170. Peter Schmidt, "When Overseeing a University System Means Defusing Lawmakers' Outrage Over Neutral Pronouns," *The Chronicle of Higher Education*, October 30, 2105, A 18.

More than 200 campuses have created "bias response teams" which have the mission of investigating complaints which may be anonymous about any incidents that may reflect "bias." Everyone has biases about one thing or another. So when is it permitted to voice them? As is true with most free speech restrictions, the definition of what speech is permissible and what can be sanctioned is blurry. Such uncertainty almost always leads to a chilling effect on clearly constitutional speech.

Even faculty and classroom assignments can be subject to scrutiny by Bias Response Teams. At the University of Northern Colorado, adjunct professor Mike Jensen assigned Greg Lukianoff's and Jonathan Haidt's book, "The Coddling of the American Mind." When the students in his class were asked to debate same sex marriage and transgender issues, a transgender woman told the campus Bias Response Team that she was "very offended and hurt by this." A UNC official then told Jensen that he could "face scrutiny" by the Equal Employment Opportunity Commission as well as Title IX and Title VII investigations. The official was recorded as saying, "If the topic's worth that, it's your call." In 2016, UNC decided to shut down its Bias Response Team, but adjunct Jensen was not rehired.

Most Bias Response Teams are focused on remarks made by students to other students. At Syracuse University bias has been defined as "name calling," "avoiding or excluding others" and "making comments on social media about someone's political affiliations or beliefs."[171] This over reaction to campus bias problems in an election year or at any time is not consistent with the speech rights of the public at large.

The University of Michigan also has a Bias Response Team which has investigated 150 incidents since 2017. UM's suggested definition of bias is "The most important indication of bias is your own feeling.[172] The perceived "bias" may be "intentional or unintentional." Students are urged to report peers, anonymously if they prefer, "and to encourage others to report if they have been the target or witness of a bias incident." The UM Bias Response Team, composed of top administrators and law enforcement officers, can also investigate off-campus speech. Students who violate the policy may be disciplined by required training sessions or even suspension or

---

171. Jeffrey Aaron Synder, "The dangers of not valuing free speech on campuses," *Inside Higher Education,* September 1, 2016.

172. Jillian Kay Melchior, "The Bias Response Team Is Watching," *The Wall Street Journal,* May 8, 2018.

expulsion. University spokeswoman, Kim Broekhuitzen, apparently able to discern the thought processes of the nearly 45,000 students enrolled at UM, declared that the Bias Response Team has operated for "a number of years, and we have certainly not seen it chill speech here." But a new organization, Speech First, composed of students, their families, and alumni, disagreed and brought a federal lawsuit alleging that the UM student code and the Bias Response Team threatened First Amendment protected speech. After the lawsuit was filed, UM changed many of its bias response definitions and policies "to ensure their consistency with principles of free speech." The trial court then refused to grant a preliminary injunction against UM, since campus had altered its policies. Speech First's Sixth Circuit appeal raises the question of whether UM should not still be judicially enjoined because its actions in changing unconstitutional practices are "capable of repetition" by future administrators after the lawsuit is over.[173]

On December 13, 2018, Speech First filed a similar law suit against a series of speech restrictions at the University of Texas, at Austin.[174] On that 52,000 student campus, the Campus Climate Response Team is empowered to investigate and sanction any perceived discrimination based on "race, color, religion, national origin, gender, gender identify, gender expression, age, disability, citizenship, veteran status, sexual orientation, ideology, political views, or political affiliation." According to UT's administrative rules, speech should be reported, if perceived as "offensive, insulting, insensitive, or derogatory" and occurring" in the classroom, on social media, at a party or student organization event."

What message are many higher educational institutions sending to students about the constitutional value of free speech? What campus administrators are being empowered to adjudicate the boundaries of what speech is permissible and what is not? What principles and due process do they follow?

While inclusion and diversity policies should mean that no one is excluded because of background, it should not preclude criticisms of the philosophies or behaviors of persons and groups. Instead of viewing campuses as an environment where robust, though civil, discussions should take place on the most important issues affecting the world and individual development, some administrators see college as one massive support

---

173. *Speech First v. Mark Schlissel,* No.18-1917.
174. *Speech First, Inc. v. Gregory L. Fenves, President* and thirty other UT officials.

group. Lee McIntyre, criticizing the tendency of campus confirmation bias leading to the disinvitation of controversial speakers, has written: "Certainty is dangerous, especially on a college campus, where ideas are supposed to be questioned. An education that shields students from discomfort turns colleges into country clubs that give credentials."[175]

Further many campus support networks are not value free, but instead reinforce with speech codes, limited free speech areas, and emphasis on microaggressions etc. what Fredrik deBoer called "The Things We Are All Already Decided" upon frameworks of argumentation.[176] No good or decent person could possibly disagree with these "Things." Given the partisan identifications of most administrators and staff, the "Things" agreed on resemble much more the platform of one party than the other.

While some campus groups are carefully protected from criticism, others are not. Labeling persons and groups as guilty of paternalism, racism, sexism, white privilege, homophobia, and xenophobia by administratively sponsored and funded advocacy campus groups is not unusual. When Smith College hosted a lively off-campus debate on the subject, "Challenging the Ideological Echo Chamber: Free Speech, Civil Discourse and the Liberal Arts," the alumnae and staff participants obviously mentioned controversial ideas and words. The Smith College newspaper later reported on the event under the title, "Backlash Follows the Use of Racial Slur at NYC Panel" and attached a warning to its published transcript "Trigger/ Content Warnings: Racism/racial slurs, ableist slurs, antisemitic language, anti-Muslim/Islamophobic language, anti-immigrant language, sexist/ misogynistic slurs, references to race-based violence, references to antisemitic violence," are contained herein.[177] University of Missouri protestors later added "adultism" and "intersextionality" to the speech garbage dump, though *The Economist* could not figure out what the latter meant.[178] Apparently if speech can be placed in one of these "ism" or "ist" garbage cans, the nuances of an argument need not be considered.

---

175. Lee McIntyre, "Willful Ignorance on Campus," *The Chronicle of Higher Education*, January 16, 2016, B5.

176. (http://frederikdeboer.com/2014/04/29). For a critical description of the research on concept of microaggressions, see Althea Nagai. "The Pseudo-Science of Microaggressions," *Academic Questions*, (Spring, 2017), Vol. 30, No 1, pp.47–57.

177. Transcription. *Smith Sophian*, October 13, 2014.

178. *The Economist*, January 21, 2016.

This kind of conformity even may be counter-productive, since, if beliefs are rarely tested, adherence may be superficial. University of Virginia President, Teresa A. Sullivan, in a speech to the American Council on Education, pointed out that, "Students can be the biggest opponents of free speech without realizing it when they demand to be free from speech they find offensive." That does them a disservice because "we're leaving them unprepared for the intellectual and social fray they will enter the moment they step off campus."[179] Perhaps this may explain why politics has become so much more about celebrities than issues for millennials which often leads them to eschew voting in non-presidential year elections.[180] Furthermore, higher education may be losing support among external constituencies such as alumni and legislators, if they feel their ideas are not represented or even debated on campus.[181] If they see a campus culture focused on demands, protests, sit-ins, and censorship, instead of a culture of debate, they may come to doubt the integrity of the academic enterprise.

Policy debates are not necessarily fun; and, if people are honest in their opinions, are often divisive, so there may be a tacit understanding not to sponsor them in order to maintain a campus as a friendly place to everyone.[182] Consequently, some campus cultures try to function like extended

179. As reported by Chris Quintana, *The Chronicle of Higher Education*, March 14, 2017.

180. Mike Maciag, "Millennials Let their Grandparents Decide Local Elections," *Governing,* January 2017.

181. According to a national fund raising organization, among 35 small selective liberal arts colleges, annual fund results were 29 percent behind 2015 in dollars and 64 percent behind in donors. Anemona Hartocollis, "College Student Protest, Alumni Fondness Fades and Checks Shrink," *The New York Times,* August 5, 2016. See also Jeremy Willinger, "Protests Rise and Donations Drop," The *Heterodox Academy* website, August 15, 2016. Steve Kolowich, "Melissa Click, U. Of Missouri Professor Who Riled Free Speech Advocates, Is Fired," *The Chronicle of Higher Education,* October 2016; Eric Kellerman, "Mizzou tries to heal its fractured relationship with Its Legislature," *The Chronicle for Higher Education*, March 4, 2016; and Thomas Lambert, "How Not to Recover From a Crisis, Mizzou Edition." http://www.jamesgmartincenter/2017/09/not-recover-crisis-mizzou-edition. The state legislature cut the University's appropriation by $22 million causing a 12% loss in the institution's operating budget and a lay-off of 307 employees. Angela Mueller, "Mizzou freshmen enrollment down 35 percent after protests." *St. Louis Business Journal,* July 10, 2017.

The after effects remained Rick Seltzer, "Missouri 3 Years Later: Lessons Learned, Protests Still Resonate," *Inside Higher Education,* September 12, 2018. See also, Ben Trachtenberg, "The University of Missouri Protests and their Lessons for Higher Education Policy and Administration," *Kentucky Law Journal* forthcoming.

182. Eric Hoover, "The Comfortable Kid," *The Chronicle of Higher Education,* July 28, 2014. See also an essay by Mark Bauerlein, "A Very Long Disengagement" about the relation-

multicultural families where identity, political, and religious disagreements are not to be discussed, lest they disrupt the desired harmony and make some feel less welcome. In the "diversity/ tolerance, inclusion culture" some administrators seem to be asserting that when any person or interest group might be offended by any expressed ideas in a classroom, in social or public media, the University should formally distance itself from that expression in the name of preserving campus civility. **Thus, it is possible that, the more diverse campuses become, the more areas of public policy will be off-limits for public debate.**

This can only lead to an atmosphere of self and prior censorship and sometimes an environment of suppressed feelings among those who feel their viewpoints or issues are never on the campus agenda. Yet, many legitimate academic decisions involving admissions, grading, scholarship awards, selection for athletic, theatrical, and musical events may seem insensitive to those affected negatively by the outcome. Professors whose research data, methodology, conclusions, and, occasionally even their integrity, are challenged by their peers may regard those expressions as insensitive, but what is the alternative in an institution that seeks to reward merit and truth-seeking?

Adding to the tolerance, inclusion, and respect agenda promoted by student affairs' offices is a concern by legal counsels that some speech might lead to a finding by the U. S. Office of Civil Rights (OCR) that a "hostile environment" for some protected groups exists on campus. The "hostile environment" concept originated in interpretations of Title VII employment law, which held that it is not enough for an employer to avoid overt acts of bias, the employer is also responsible for the environment that might be created by employees or even customers.[183]

This concept has migrated to campuses which are enjoined to avoid actions or speech that might lead to a hostile learning environment for any group. Thus, it may seem better to avoid publicly discussing divergent ideas about affirmative action, illegal immigration, same sex marriage,

---

ship of students' entertainment choices and their lack of civic knowledge and engagement. *The Chronicle of Higher Education*, January 6, 2006.

183. Eugene Volokh, "What Speech Hostile Work Environment, Harassment Law Restrict," 85 *Georgetown Law Journal*, 1997; also by the same author, "How Harassment Law Restricts Free Speech," 47 *Rutgers Law Journal*, 561 (1995) and "Thinking Ahead About Freedom of Speech and "Hostile Work Environment" Harassment," 17 *Berkeley Journal of Employment and Labor Law*, (1996).

and rape cultures etc., because if a speaker criticizes any of those concepts, the campus can be accused of creating a hostile learning environment for some segment of its students or employees. In fact, however, in none of the controversies over free speech or debate, did campus authorities cite any specific findings or documents by legal counsel or government agencies to justify their decision to favor some students/customers seeking to suppress speech of others. An attitude of better to be safe than sorry seems to have dominated administrative thinking.

In 2018, however, the OCR re-opened a complaint against Rutgers University for permitting a hostile environment for Jewish students as an ethnic group after a supporter of the movement to boycott Israel spoke at the University in 2011.[184] OCR does not have jurisdiction over religious discrimination and its view that religious and secular Jews form a single ethnic group is controversial. The Obama Administration previously rejected the complaint and the Trump administration had generally been in favor of reducing federal regulation of education, so the new investigation surprised some people. Rutgers has about 69,000 students on its three campuses, so the complaint raises the issue of when a single speaker can create a hostile environment against a campus group. A more difficult question is when there is a departmental consensus on campus critical of a group, such as has been the case of several disciplinary associations that supported the Boycott, Divest, Sanction movement which calls for actions against Israeli scholars and institutions. But does inviting an individual speaker who opposes Black Lives Matter or who criticizes white privilege, for example, create a hostile environment? There are those left and right on campus who would seize on that concept to shut down speech they do not like. What if Rutgers had sponsored a debate on "Can the interests of Palestinians and Jews be equally accommodated in Israel?" The debate might be controversial, depending on the speakers chosen, but in legal terms would that create a hostile environment?

(3) Campus cultures vary widely; but where course work, grades and careers are not directly affected, these cultures often reflect the need to make college a fun experience for the customers. Thus, there is a great emphasis

---

184. Erica L Green, "Education Depart Reopens Rutgers Case Charging Discrimination Against Jewish Students," *New York Times*, September 11, 2018. Andrew Kreighbaum," Limiting the Debate," *Inside Higher Education*, September 13, 2018. Both the ACLU and F.I.R.E criticized the OCR action.

on student living and recreational amenities,[185] athletic, and other entertainment spectacles. A focus on the student as consumer may drain attention from academic and citizenship preparation activities.[186] Craig Meister, who founded an admissions consulting firm, Admissions Intel, advises parents to be certain their children will like the environment where they will spend four or more years of their lives. He points out, however, that "Today many colleges are upping their institutions' housing and amenities. Dorms are cozier, gyms are state-of-art, and gluten-free food is served in the dining halls. In the industry, we call it 'Club Ed.' No longer is it just about a degree, but it is also about the experience."[187]

(4) Why do so few faculty, who should have the most at stake in protecting academic freedom and intellectual diversity, actively promote public policy debates? Why are certain topics, while debated nationally, considered untouchable and rarely appear on the menu of campus events at all?

Faculty incentives and ideologies do not incline most faculty to sponsor or participate in on-campus debates. On most campuses with a research mission, faculty are promoted and otherwise rewarded for obtaining grants and contracts and publishing in peer reviewed journals.[188] In many disciplines, the public policy implications of this work are marginal and citizenship preparation, unlike job preparation, is not seen as a goal. Sponsoring or participating in public policy discussions is a time-consuming distraction for most faculty. Better to exchange emails or journal comments with professional colleagues than engage in face-to-face debates on campus away from the sheltered sanctuaries of the classroom. Given existing re-

---

185. Scott Carlson, "Spending Shifts as Colleges Compete on Students' Comfort," *The Chronicle of Higher Education,* July 28, 2014.

186. Brad Wolverton, Ben Hallman, Shane Shifflett and Sandhya Kambhampati, "The $10-Billion Sports Tab: How College Students are Funding the Athletics Arms Race," *The Chronicle for Higher Education,*" November 15, 2015.

187. Meister as quoted by Alice Shapin, "Mission Mortarboard," *Baltimore Magazine,* September 2016, pp. 67–8.

188. An interesting discussion about faculty reward systems and the decline of public intellectuals with campus appointments can be found in Alan Wolfe, "The Vanishing Big Thinker," *The Chronicle of Higher Education,* August 5, 2016, p.B-6–9. Wolfe wrote, "The academic job market and tenure expectations focus more intently on publications... that tend to stress contributions to scholarship over participation in public discussions." See also: Phillip Joyce, "How Academia is Failing Government: Because the incentives for academic research are misaligned, it has little impact on the real world of public administration and policy." *Governing.* August 31, 2016.

ward systems on many campuses, faculty have reduced their traditional roles as mentors in the overall intellectual development of their students.

(5) Another factor is that on many campuses, the faculty, particularly in the social science and humanities disciplines most relevant to public policy, are quite politically and ideologically homogenous. **It would be an oversimplification to assert that this faculty homogeneity is the sole cause of the paucity of campus policy debates, but it would be worth investigating whether the dominant ideological factions see the necessity or advantage in sponsoring policy debates that would challenge their viewpoints.**

The American Council of Education (ACE), together with dozens of other higher education associations, issued a joint statement on intellectual diversity in 2005.[189] The ACE statement declared in lofty terms that "Intellectual pluralism and academic freedom are central principles of American Higher Education," but then added language that created lots of wiggle room: "Individual campuses must give meaning and definition to these concerns within the context of disciplinary standards and institutional mission." Four years later, the American Council of Trustees and Alumni followed up with a pamphlet illustrating some campus affirmations of the concept of "intellectual diversity,"[190] but unless there is some way to measure and report on the events institutions actually sponsor for their students, the concept may be just one more higher education buzzword.

The pervasive emphasis on obtaining diversity in race and gender or on how faculty *look* may obscure the reality that there is little diversity in how faculty *think* about important political, economic, and social policies. Almost any campus administration can instantly provide statistics about the race and gender composition of their faculty, but very few administrations are interested in knowing or caring how many faculty are Democrats, Republicans, Marxists, libertarians, conservatives, religious or

---

189. American Council on Education, "Statement of Academic Rights and Responsibilities," June, 2005. See also American Council of Trustees and Alumni, "Intellectual Diversity: Time for Action." December 2005.

190. American Council of Trustees and Alumni, "Protecting the Free Exchange of Ideas: How Trustees Can Advance Intellectual Diversity on Campus," 2009. For example, Anthony Marx, the President of Amherst College announced: "To expose the College community to diverse perspectives, the President's office has organized a series of talks that pair speakers of divergent perspectives to discuss the important issues of the day." p. 28.

feminists. Whether whole departments have uniform views on important policy questions is rarely examined on campuses.[191]

When Everett Ladd and Seymour Lipset published *The Divided Academy* in 1975, they found that 37% of the faculty over age 55 identified as Republicans, while only 18% under 35 so identified[192] A national survey in 2005 found that overall 72 percent of faculty described themselves as liberals and only 15 percent as conservatives, but that in English literature, philosophy, political science, and religious studies departments at least 80 percent of the faculty considered themselves liberal and no more than 5 percent thought of themselves as conservative.[193] Elite institutions may be even more one sided. When economist Karl Zinsmeister published findings in 2005 on political affiliations of Stanford University and the University of California Berkeley faculty, he found that the ratio of Democrats to Republicans was 8 to 1 or 10 to 1. The ratio of Democrats to Republicans was 28 to 1 for sociologists and 30 to 1 for anthropologists.[194] There are also considerable differences by region, where New England faculty are by far the most liberal, while professors in the Rocky Mountain region were less so.[195]

The political affiliations of faculty in economics, history, journalism/communications, law and psychology at elite institutions has been remeasured in 2016 using the Voting Lists Online Aristotle link. Overall, the research showed professors registered as Democrats outnumber Republicans

191. For a review of the literature on faculty political affiliations, see Scott Jaschik, "Professors and Politics: What the Research Says," *Inside Higher Education*, February 27, 2017. The issues are not whether the imbalance exists, but what causes it and how it is manifested in the various choices faculty make in performing their roles. See also Jon A. Shields and Joshua M. Dunn Sr., *Passing on the Right: Conservative Professors in the Progressive University* (New York: Oxford University Press, 2016).

192. As portrayed in Howard R. Bowen and Jack H. Schuster, *American Professors: A Natural Resource Imperiled* (New York: Oxford University Press, 1986), p. 42.

193. Howard Kuntz, "College Faculties: A Most Liberal Lot, A Study Finds," *Federalist Society*, March 29, 2005. The study reported on was by Stanley Rothman, S. Robert Lichter, and Neil Nevitte, "Politics and Professional Advancement Among College Faculty," *The Forum*, vol.3. no1, article 2, (2005) 5, http://www.bepress.com/forum/vol.3/iss1/art2).

194. Karl Zinsmeister, "Case Closed," *The American Enterprise*, January February, 2005, 42.

195. Samuel J. Abrams, "There are Conservative Professors, Just not in These States," *New York Times Sunday Review*, July1, 2016 and Sam Abrams, "The Blue Shift of the New England Professoriate," *The Heterodox Academy* website, July 6, 2016. There is apparently a shift in the political affiliations of British professors as well toward the Labour or Green parties away from the Conservative party. Noah Carl, "New Report on the Political Views of the British Academics." *The Heterodox Academy* website. March 6, 2017.

by 11.5 to 1. There were striking differences on particular campuses. At Pepperdine the ratio was 1:2 Democrats to 1 Republicans and at Ohio State is was 3.2 Democrats to 1 Republicans, but at institutions with high profile professional and graduate programs in those fields the ratios were Harvard 10:1, Stanford 11:1, Duke 11:1, Cornell 13:1, UC-Berkeley 14:1, NYU 16:1, Yale 16:1, MIT 19:1, Maryland 26:1, Princeton 30:1, Columbia 30:1, Johns Hopkins 35.1, and Brown 60.1.[196]

A more recent report of research by Mitchell Langbert found that in sociology departments at top national liberal arts colleges, the Democrat to Republican ratio was 43.8 to 1, while in departments of anthropology it was 56 to 0. In the anthropology departments of the 66 top liberal arts colleges ranked by *U.S. News*, there was not a single registered Republican.[197] Yet these are not fields in which scientific certainty can be fixed, but are study areas in which multiple perspectives should be welcomed.

Partisan identification does not reflect complete single-mindedness about issues, since there are internal debates within parties. Partisan affiliation, however, does generally indicate that some policy alternatives are not acceptable or even debatable. If all the members of an academic department hold the same partisan identities, it should raise questions about whether students will be exposed to the various policy alternatives debated beyond the campus. Partisan homogeneity may also affect faculty decisions about curriculum, invited speakers, internships and even letters of recommendation.[198]

Cass R. Sunstein, former Professor of Law at Harvard and Chicago and Obama White House official, commented on the partisan imbalance in higher education that Langbert and others have documented:

> For two reasons, these numbers, and others like them are genuinely disturbing. The first involves potential discrimination on the part of educational institutions. Some departments might be disinclined to

---

196. Mitchell Langbert, Anthony J. Quain, and Daniel B. Klein, "Faculty Voting Registration in Economics, History, Journalism, Law and Psychology," *Economic Journal Watch*, Vol.13. No.3, p.424.

197. Mitchell Langbert, "Homogenous: The Political Affiliations of Elite Liberal Arts College Faculty," *Academic Questions* 31, no. 2 (Summer 2018).

198. For a discussion of why the conservative/liberal imbalance appears among higher education faculty, see George Yancey, "The Academic Reason Why There Are So Few Conservatives in Academia," and the forty comments that followed. *Patheos*, November 18, 2017.

hire potential faculty members based on their political convictions. Such discrimination might take the form of unconscious devaluation of people whose views do not fit the dominant perspective.... talented people might not pursue academic careers at all, because they expect their potential professors will not appreciate their work. The second reason is that students are less likely to get a good education, and faculty members are likely to learn less from one another, if there is a prevailing orthodoxy. Students and faculty might end up in a kind of information cocoon.[199]

Sunstein suggests as a remedy to these problems:

Those who teach in departments lacking intellectual diversity have an obligation to offer competing views and to present them fairly and with respect. Second, those who run departments lacking ideological diversity have an obligation to find people who represent competing views-visiting speakers, visiting professors and new hires.[200]

Surely, these are responsibilities for serious educators. But they are not new responsibilities, so why can we expect higher education to make necessary changes now?

Partisan imbalance may also affect the ideologies and behaviors of professors in professional schools. Even in law schools that often sponsor debates and forums on some topics, the faculty are not representative in either racial, religious or partisan terms and recent recruitment patterns are reinforcing the trends of fewer whites, Christians or Republicans than availability data would suggest should be the case.[201] James C. Phillips has asked the question "Why are there so few Conservatives and Libertarians in Legal Academia: An Empirical Exploration of Three Hypotheses?" and concluded that it is not because professors identified with these groups are less qualified, productive or frequently cited.[202] In 2005, Professor John O. McGinnis published a paper in the *Georgetown Law Journal* recording

---

199. Cass R. Sunstein, "The Problem With All Those Liberal Professors," Bloomberg, September 17, 2018.

200. Ibid.

201. James Lindgren "Measuring Diversity: Law Faculties in 1997 and 2013,"*Harvard Journal of Law and Public Policy*, Vol. 39, No.1, Winter 2016).

202. Ibid, pp. 154–208.

the partisan contributions of faculty at the top 21 law schools.[203] Of those that gave at least $200 to federal campaigns, 81 percent gave wholly or predominantly to Democrats, while just 15 percent gave to Republicans. Not surprisingly, when these professors joined in open letters on political and legal matters, their comments followed partisan lines.

There is a widespread consensus in higher education that faculty hiring should be non-discriminatory given various federal and state laws,[204] while seeking simultaneously to increase "diversity." If diversity is defined narrowly in race, ethnic, and gender terms and operationalized to create preferences in search procedures, non-discrimination and "diversity" may not be consistent goals. Job advertisements often state "women and minorities are encouraged to apply," so, then, who is not encouraged to apply? Whether non-discrimination and diversity are compatible depends on the institutional definition of "diversity, the administrative tools used to enforce these definitions, and how officials know when enough "diversity" exists. On the other hand, if "diversity" is defined in terms of multiplying intellectual viewpoints and encouraging well-balanced departmental research agendas and public events, then the search for added diversity may be quite defensible legally and educationally sound. Behind the "diversity" mantra, there may be quite explicit political goals that may contribute to the partisan imbalance among contemporary faculty.[205]

In a 2016 *Inside Higher Education* essay, Tanya Golash-Boza, Associate Professor of Sociology at the University of California at Merced, and author of *Deported: Immigrant Policing, Disposable Labor and Global Capitalism* (NYU Press, 2015), suggested tips on "How to write an effective diversity statement."[206] She noted "Faculty job postings are increasingly asking for diversity statements, in addition to research and teaching descriptions."

---

203. John O. McGinnis et al, "The Patterns and implications of Political Contributions by Elite Law School Faculty," 93 *Geo L.J.*1167, 1187 (2005).

204. The Equal Protection Clause of the 14th Amendment, Title VI of the Civil Rights Act of 1964, Title IX of the Educational Amendments of 1972 and Section 504 of the Rehabilitation Act of 1973. Discrimination on the basis of partisan identification is currently not illegal, but at public universities, if such discrimination could be proven, it might raise First Amendment questions.

205. This issue was first explored by the author in "Diversity and Exclusion," *Academic Questions*, Vol. 31, Issue 3, 2018.

206. Tanya Golash-Boza, "How to Write an Effective Diversity Statement," *Inside Higher Education*, June 10, 2016, https://www.insidehighered.com/advice/2016/06/10/how-write-effective-diversity-statement-essay.

The University of California at San Diego, for example, declares, "The purpose of the statement is to identify candidates who have professional skill, experience, or willingness to engage in activities that would enhance campus diversity and equity efforts." Golash-Boza acknowledged:

> Diversity statements are relatively new additions to the job application packet. Thus, search committees are still developing assessment tools for such statements, and many campuses lack clear guidelines. Nevertheless, you can use this novelty to your advantage by writing a stellar statement that emphasizes your record of contributions to diversity and equity as well as your commitment to future efforts.

Among her specific pieces of advice were to empathize with students who were disadvantaged, confess to your own privilege, focus on commonly accepted understandings of diversity and equity (race, gender, social class and sexual orientation), and write about your commitment to achieving equality and enhancing diversity.

A year later, Victoria Reyes, Assistant Professor of Sociology at the University of California, Riverside, followed up with another *Inside Higher Education* essay on effective diversity statements.[207] She wrote if you are underrepresented in a particular way, that should be stated, but it is not enough. Instead, you should model your research statement after guidelines issued by the National Center for Institutional Diversity at the University of Michigan:

> Inform our understanding of systems of power and privilege and their interactions with groups historically underrepresented and marginalized based on identities, including but not limited to race, ethnicities, gender, social/economic class, culture, sexual identity, ability status and religion.
>
> Highlight the experiences of disenfranchised populations, whose narratives have traditionally been relegated to the outer periphery of intellectual inquiry and academic scholarship, made invisible through epistemologies and research methods that privilege dominant social groups.

---

207. Victoria Reyes, "Demystifying the Diversity Statement," *Inside Higher Education*, January 25, 2018.

Foreground the knowledge systems, assets and resources, and cultural strengths of members of historically marginalized communities in order to promote empowerment of individuals and groups from these communities.

Whether this admonition reflects a defensible view of American society or not, the guidelines clearly embody a particular political perspective. Prospective candidates are expected to subscribe to them not only in their initial research and teaching, but also in their long term commitments to fulfill institutional diversity mandates. Suppose, instead of screening job applicants for their commitment to diversity and equity, the required political values were "respect for traditional American values and limited government"? Who then would be preferred on ideological grounds?

Screening in some candidates for their political attitudes means screening out others. When this happens the pursuit of diversity does not mean inclusion, but exclusion. Sometimes the inclusion agenda means seeking proportional representation of underrepresented groups in all campus functions. If vigorously implemented, this can also mean exclusion of the "overrepresented" as well. Both the Golash-Boza and Reyes essays were written by sociologists who did not acknowledge that the political goals they were advocating would serve to reinforce the already dominant ideological views in their field, creating little new intellectual diversity for students.[208]

Ideological imbalance may also affect behavior as well. A 2007 study found that 53% percent of university professors sampled had a cool or

---

208. The program for International Sociological Association World Congress of Sociology held in Toronto, July 15–21, 2018 reads: "Since the inception of the discipline, sociologists have been concerned with power, violence and justice. Current social, economic and political challenges enhance their relevance. As capitalist globalization expands and deepens, corporate power increases along with global, national and local inequalities. New geo-political power configurations and confrontations are emerging, with violence being used as a tool to oppress and resist oppression." The June 2018 issue of *The American Sociologist* has an important discussion of the political values in the discipline. See particularly, the results of a survey of 479 sociologists which showed that commitment to the fields of "moral mission," preferred research paradigm, gender, and political orientation predict sociologists' viewpoints. Authors Mark Horowitz, Anthony L. Haynor, and Kenneth Kickham concluded: "The results, we suggest, can be understood by conceptualizing the field of sociology as an "emotive community". . . . "Sociology's Sacred Victims and the Politics of Knowledge: Moral Foundations Theory and Disciplinary Controversies."

negative attitude toward evangelicals, though it is unlikely any campus implementing a diversity policy has taken steps to protect such students or job applicants. A 2012 study found that 82% of liberal social psychologists, who constitute the vast majority of that discipline, acknowledge that they would be at least a little prejudiced against a conservative applicant for a departmental job.[209]

If the faculty are unionized, their organizations may sometimes take positions that bring politics into teaching. After the 2016 election, the New York's Professional Staff Congress (PSC) urged CUNY professors to "teach resistance" and to publicly affirm that they would "integrate" into class instruction "how President Trump's policies affect [their] area of scholarship and ask their students how they are affected." When in 2018, the Supreme Court found in *Janus v. AFSCME* that being required to pay union dues was "compelled speech" in violation of the First Amendment, the PSC denounced the decision for supporting "an agenda that has been planned and lavishly supported by billionaires and far-right organizations. Its goal is to undo every gain made by workers, people of color, immigrants, women, the middle class and the poor during the last half-century."[210] Under this union guidance, students may not be exposed to fundamental differences of opinion, even if some campus forums occur.[211]

Some disciplines are more politically relevant than others, so generalizations about faculty political identifications as a whole may not be helpful in understanding the actual political discourse students hear in classrooms or on campus generally. For example, Smith, Mayer, and Fritschler found that of those faculty with partisan identifications, 56% were aligned with the Democrat party, while only 14% were Republicans, but more natural sciences faculty classified themselves as independents than those in the social sciences or humanities. On the other hand, their survey of college faculty found that, although they were overwhelmingly Democrats, those polled did not believe that affiliation affected hiring decisions or the political climate on campus.[212] The report on survey responses to possible ideological

209. Jose L. Durate et.al. "Political Diversity Will Improve Social Psychological Science," *Behavioral and Brain Sciences* (Cambridge University Press, 2014).

210. KC Johnson, "Janus and the Campus," *City Journal*, July 1, 2018.

211. ACTA, "Intellectual Diversity," 3.

212. Jeremy Myers, Bruce L.R. Smith and A. Lee Fritschler, *Closed Minds? Politics and Ideology in American Universities* (Washington, D.C.: The Brookings Institution, 2008). pp.71–91. Table 5-8–5-11. The gateway question asked was how faculty handled political

discrimination did not disaggregate by discipline or type of campus, so the aggregate response may mask some problems, if the question had been defined more narrowly. The authors reported that sociologists reported a Democrat partisan affiliation to a Republican affiliation by a 28 to 1 ratio, while among mathematicians the ratio was a little more than 2 to 1. Mathematicians may accurately report politics has little effect on their academic decisions, while sociologists may view the problem differently. Furthermore, without other confirmation, simply asking faculty whether their political identifications affect their judgment and decisions may not be definitive proof.

While the *Closed Minds* 2008 survey showed that professors did not feel that faculty political affiliations affected their campuses' political climate, three 2017 student surveys showed a different picture. A Cato Free Speech and Tolerance Survey of undergraduate and graduate students found 72% of Republican students said their campuses' political climate prevented them from sharing their political views. Even 70% of Independents felt the same way, as did 51% of students who identified as Democrats. Only students who identified as "very liberal" did not feel the need to self-censor.[213] In a different survey of 1,227 currently enrolled college students, 53% reported they did not think their institutions frequently "encourages students to consider a wide variety of viewpoints and perspectives." Students, in particular, were reluctant to discuss race and gender, with conservatives the most fearful.[214] Another data base, describing student attitudes toward viewpoint diversity comes from the 2017 National Survey of Student Engagement (NSSE) "Inclusiveness and engagement and cultural diversity module." Students reported that their institutions actively supported racial, ethnic, sexual orientation, and gender diversity, but far less so for po-

---

questions in their classes. Of the 1,154 respondents, 61% said that 'Politics seldom comes up in their classes because of the nature of the subject I teach." p.84. So the most relevant analysis would be about the way professors who did handle politically sensitive issues acted in classroom settings. That analysis was not made. Nor was the question asked about whether political ideology in the politically relevant disciplines affects what research is funded and/ or published or affects which speakers are invited to campus or what topics are discussed in open campus forums.

213. Emily Ekins, "20% of College Students say College Faculty Has Balanced Mix of Political Views." November 6, 2017. https://www.cato.org/blog/20-current-students-say-college-faculty-has-balanced-mix-political-views

214. Sean Stevens, "The Campus Expression Survey, Summary of New Data", https://heterodoxacademy.org.2017/12/the-campus-expression-survey.

litical diversity.[215] The empirical results from this research about the lack of debate or forums with divergent viewpoints are consistent with these surveyed student perceptions.

Also in 2017, John Villasensor of the Brooking Institution conducted a national survey of 1,500 current undergraduate students from 49 states and the District of Columbia about their views about speech.[216] Regarding the question of whether the First Amendment protects "hate speech," most who had an opinion said "no," but the striking difference was that 49% of females said "no" compared to only 38% of males. With regard to shouting down a speaker (where no background or topic was stated), but which some students opposed for unknown reasons, a slender majority agreed with that action. But the partisan differences were substantial. Among students who identified as Democrats, 62% agreed with preventing the audience from hearing the speech, while only 39% of the Republicans agreed. In this case, females were less likely to agree than males. If the protests involved violence, about 20% of all students would condone that activity, with males much more likely than females to support violence. In a further question, students were given the option of choosing a campus that "creates a positive learning environment for all students by prohibiting certain speech of expression of viewpoints that are offensive or biased against certain groups of people." (Option 1) or "create an open learning environment where students are exposed to all types of speech and viewpoints, even if it means allowing speech that is offensive or biased against certain groups of people."(Option 2). Overall, 53% choose Option 1 with some significant partisan differences; 61% of Democrats chose Option 1, while 53% of Republicans chose Option 2. It would be interesting to know whether the divides in student opinion actually reflect partisan identifications or race, ethnic and gender preference identifications. Whatever the source of the misunderstandings about the scope of the First Amendment, Villasenor points out that "What happens on campuses often foreshadows broader societal trends. Today's college students are tomorrow's attorneys, teachers, professors, policymakers, legislators and judges."

He concludes:

---

215. Samuel J, Abrams, "Many students embrace viewpoint diversity. Why Won't Colleges?" *Real Clear Education*, https://realcleareducation.com/articles/2017/12/15/many-students.

216. John Villasenor, "Views among colleges students regarding the First Amendment: Results from a new survey," Brookings Instruction, September 18, 2017.

The survey results establish with data what has been clear anecdotally to anyone who has been observing campus dynamics in recent years. Freedom of expression is deeply imperiled on U.S. campuses. In fact, despite protestations to the contrary (often with statements like "we fully support the First Amendment, but. . .") freedom of expression is clearly not, in practice available on many campuses, including many public campuses that have first Amendment obligations.[217]

The public skepticism about the role of free speech on campuses is reflected in a representative national survey of adults conducted by the Freedom Forum Institute's "2018 State of the First Amendment" report. Only 56% of the respondents knew that freedom of speech was a part of the First Amendment, though that was higher than the percentages that knew that The Right to Assemble (12%), Freedom of the Press (13%) and Freedom of Religion (15%) were protected there. More specifically, 51% of the respondents thought colleges should be able to retract invitations to controversial speakers who would provoke large scale student protests or 47% if the speaker might be likely to offend some groups or individuals.[218]

Given the attitudes of many students toward speech they dislike and the lack of understanding of free speech in the general public, it is certainly

---

217. Ibid., p. 2. A survey taken of the general public showed some of the same ambiguity about freedom of speech. Substantial majorities of Democrats said sexist or racist offensive speech should be restricted, while Republicans were more permissive. On the other hand, Republicans were more sympathetic to having colleges being able to restrict "the teaching of radical ideas," while independents and Democrats less so. Chris Ellis, the lead author of the Bucknell University Institute for Public Policy survey concluded that was unfair to imply that an entire generation supports disrupting speech, but that "it's a small and loud group of students" who disrupt, "but most students are much more willing to engage in different perspectives." Scott Jaschik, "Study suggests it's not just students who have difficulty understanding free expression," *Inside Higher Education,* November 10, 2017. See also Oliver Traldi, "Don't be fooled: There is a free speech Crisis," *The Chronicle of Higher Education,* April 23, 2018. See also; Janet Napolitano, "It's is time to free speech on campus again," *The Boston Globe,* October 2, 2016. Also see Frederick M. Hess and Grant Addison, "Restoring Free Inquiry on Campus," *National Affairs,* Spring, 2018.

218. Freedom Forum Institute, "The 2018 State of the First Amendment" pp. 3–7. There seems to be some spillover in attitudes about free speech on the campus and in the social media, where so many experience speech in all forms. According to the survey, 77% thought social media companies should remove "hate speech" and 68% believed that "personal attacks" should be deleted from their websites, though the respondents were evenly divided about whether governments should require social media sites to monitor and remove "objectionable content."

understandable that administrators will not want to court controversy and possible disruption on their campuses. In acquiescing to the attitudes and unstated threats among students recorded in the Brookings survey, however, administrators legitimate suppressing ideas outside the existing campus consensus on public policy.

Walter Kimbrough, former President at Philander Smith College and now at Arkansas Baptist College, candidly affirmed that anxiety: "When we shut down speech, there will be losers. Many of those losers will be the ones whose brilliance will go unnoticed without an opportunity to skillfully argue for what they believe." But he also concluded:

> I'll admit. I'm scared. The robust discussion I have always sought to expose my students to doesn't seem to be worth it anymore. It feels as if the best thing to do is to play safe and simply invite either entertainers or athletes to speak as feel-good events or hard-core academics whose presence will go unnoticed.[219]

For undergraduate audiences, the problem of the lack of intellectual diversity about public policy issues was recently raised by John Etchemendy, former Stanford Provost, in a speech to his University's Board of Trustees. While his whole speech is worth reading, his most salient points are:

> Over the years I have watched a growing intolerance at universities in this country. Not intolerance along racial or ethnic or gender lines—there, we have made laudable progress. Rather, a kind of intellectual intolerance [exists], a political one-sidedness, that is the antithesis of what universities should stand for. It manifests itself in many ways: in the intellectual monocultures that have taken over certain disciplines; in the demands to disinvite speakers and outlaw groups whose views we find offensive; in constant calls for the university itself to take political positions. We decry certain news outlets as echo chambers, while we fail to notice the echo chambers we have built around ourselves. . . . The university is not a megaphone to amplify this or that political view and when it does it violates a core mission.[220]

---

219. Walter Kimbrough, "When Debate Dies, Who Loses," *The Chronicle of Higher Education,* March 23, 2017.

220. John Etchemendy, "The Threat from Within," *The Chronicle of Higher Education,* March 17, 2017. For an opposing viewpoint in the same *Chronicle* edition, see Todd Gitlin,

Perhaps as a consequence of Etchemendy's admonition, in 2018 Stanford, the Hoover Institution and the Freeman Spogli Institute for International Studies began a program titled Cardinal Conversations. The goal is a series of discussions with well-known individuals who hold contrasting views on controversial subjects. Stanford President Marc Tessler-Lavigne and new Provost Persis Drell, added, "In both research and education, breakthroughs in understanding come not from considering a familiar, limited range of ideas, but from considering a broad range of ideas, including those we might find objectionable, and engaging in rigorous tests of them through analysis and debate."[221] Students from a wide variety of organizational backgrounds chose the topics which will include "Technology and Politics," "Inequality and Populism," and "Real and Fake News."

Ideological and partisan imbalances may affect the next generation of scholars. Higher education has been greatly concerned about the under representation of some minority groups and women in various disciplines. Search procedures, committees, and even salary offers have been restructured to remedy this problem. Study after study has been devoted to understanding this kind of racial and/or gender under representation, but there has been very little administrative attention paid to imbalances of worldviews and research agendas in various departments. There has been some speculation that bright young conservatives may be more attracted to corporate life than academia. That might be true, but why would a promising junior conservative or libertarian scholar be optimistic about a long career in an elite social science department where he or she would be dependent on colleagues for letters of recommendation, research support, and ultimately tenure? The treatment of scholars who have been disinvited or harassed as campus speakers may have a chilling effect on others considering an academic career. Charles Murray, despite being one of America's most widely published public intellectuals confronting important issues of the political implications of class, race and gender, is not a welcomed in many

---

"Reason's Last Stand," who argues that universities should be active in "standing for cosmopolitan values" and should actually put up "public interest" advertising on policy issues on billboards. Such political commitments by institutions, however, may stifle policy debates on campus.

221. Stanford News, "Stanford launched Cardinal Conversations initiative to expose campus to diverse views," January 10, 2018.

parts of the academic world, even to be debated. His conclusions are controversial, but would surely create a lively dialogue wherever presented.[222]

The reality of the partisan imbalance among faculty, administrators, and campus speakers may have finally reached public perceptions as well. In a Gallup survey of campus presidents, a majority responded they believed that the 2016 election exposed a disconnect between academe and much of American society and 70% responded that there was a growth in anti-intellectualism in the United States.[223] One newspaper editorialized "This is a culture war that only produces losers" and then captioned its comments as "Higher education haters: Why must Republicans wage war on colleges and universities?"[224] It is possible that Congressional Republican proposals to tax very large university endowments and graduate student benefits may be influenced by their perception that these types of universities are hostile generally to their party's policies.

For higher education institutions that must seek support from Red state legislatures, Congress, and federal administrative agencies, this is an ominous trend in public opinion that needs to be reckoned with.[225] The failure to debate policy issues on campus may have some long-term damaging consequences for higher education. A 2018 Gallup poll found only 48% of American adults have "a great deal" or "quite a lot" of confidence in higher education. That percentage has dropped from 57% in 2015. There was a decline in support among Democrats (6%), Independents (4%), but the

---

222. Even before the Middlebury imbroglio, a lecture he was invited to give at Azusa Pacific University in 2014 was "postponed" because of his past research was on human group differences. See "Charles Murray Questions Azusa Pacific," *Inside Higher Education*, October 17, 2014; Charles Murray, "An Open Letter to the students at Azusa Pacific University," *AEI Ideas*. American Enterprise Institute. October 17, 2014. In 2016, Murray overcame an attempt to disinvite him at Virginia Tech, though President Tim Sands wrote before Murray spoke that his work was "discredited," "flawed" and used by some to justify fascism, racism, and eugenics," and was "regarded by some in our community as repugnant, offensive and even fraudulent." Shortly thereafter, James Riley, an African-American, *a Wall Street Journal* columnist and Manhattan Institute senior fellow, was disinvited from giving the BB&T Distinguished Lecture at Tech. Peter Wood and Rachelle Peterson, "Jason Riley Is the Latest Conservative to be Disinvited from a College Campus." *National Review,* May 2, 2016.

223. "College Presidents see disconnect with public, worry about Washington," *Inside Higher Education*, March 10, 2017.

224. *Baltimore Sun,* July 13, 2017.

225. A case study of this problem in one state can be found in Ben Foster, "Disconnect: Kentucky and the Political Ideology of its Public Universities." *Academic Questions,* Fall 2018. Vol 31, No.4 pp.313–312.

greatest decline was among Republicans (17%).[226] While it is impossible to determine the exact cause of changes in public opinion to a generic question, it is not implausible that the drop in support, especially among Republicans, is related to a feeling that their viewpoints are not heard on campuses. After noting dissatisfactions about the cost of higher education and excessive interest in rankings, Lawrence S. Bacow, the new President of Harvard University, said in his 2018 inaugural address that "More persons than we would like to admit believe that universities are not nearly as open to ideas across the political spectrum as we should be."[227]

Open debates on public policy are one way to restore public confidence. Roger Williams University President Donald J. Farish commented on the partisan divide about higher education:

> If colleges campuses are being targeted as battlegrounds between extremists on the left and right, then college presidents have to find ways to reclaim the middle ground. This starts with conversations between the institution's administration and campus political groups and the creation of forums for debate between representative voices from left and right. A true debate, where students are invited to witness a meaningful presentation of opposing views, is far more useful interesting and useful than one-sided diatribes.[228]

As this research has shown, however, such debates on campus are rare. There are many different perspectives about what to do if there is ideological conformity on a campus or in a cluster of departments, if the problem is recognized at all.

Mitchell Langbert, whose valuable empirical study of faculty political homogeneity in top national liberal arts colleges (Amherst, Middlebury, Scripps, Wesleyan, and Williams), many of which were sites where speakers

---

226. Scott Jaschik, "Falling Confidence in Higher Ed," *Inside Higher Education,* October 9, 2018. A Pew Research Center poll question about whether higher education had a positive or negative impact on the country also showed that Republican perceptions had shifted from 54 percent positive in 2015 to 58 percent negative in 2017. On the other hand, the positive numbers among Democrats moved from 65 percent positive to 72 percent positive in that same period.

227. As quoted in Jachik, "Falling Confidence in Higher Ed."

228. "College Presidents see disconnect with public...," *Inside Higher Education,* March 10, 2017.

were disinvited or harassed, has suggested the problem at these institutions is irremediable and the only future course is to begin new campuses. Given the very challenging future for small underfunded private institutions, creating new ones would have a very marginal impact on the larger higher education problem.

Tom Lindsay, Director of the Center for Educational Innovation at the Texas Public Policy Foundation, argues that federal funding of higher education, coupled with the power of accrediting agencies has influenced the politicization of campuses.[229] That is an easier argument to make at the K-12 level where federal spending levers have been used to promote a number of political goals of particular administrations. But the effect of federal funding in higher education as a cause of faculty political homogeneity is not so easy to discern, except for setting priorities for various research projects. In the public sector, at least states probably already have the authority to set policies about free speech and debate, if they are wise enough to do it in ways that enlist academic allies.

David Randall, Director of Communications for the National Association of Scholars, believes that a solution might be to make universities responsible for defaults on student loans, thus reducing the numbers of students who required remedial education and the college bureaucrats who exist to service their needs. He believes these officials use a politicized lens in their programs and that remedial students are more likely to major in various identity studies that make them intolerant of views that challenge their predispositions of the proper allocation of identities and rewards. Whether institutional co-responsibility for student loans is a politically possible alternative is uncertain and there are probably more direct solutions to insuring campus freedom of speech.

Jennifer Kabbany, Editor of *The College Fix*, asserts regarding politicization that "Higher education is past the point of no return." Her solution is to use parental guidance to inoculate children from indoctrination before they set foot on campus as she has done with her son, an eighteen- year old Marine. There are important questions about the scalability of that solution and whether, given higher education's professed values, it should even be necessary.

---

229. Lindsay's essay and those of Randall, Kabbany, Schalin, Mashek, and Hyman can be found on the Martin Center website, May 9, 2018.

Jay Schalin, Director of Policy Analysis at the James G. Martin Center for Academic Renewal, thinks the key is the creation of independent alumni organizations that can penetrate administrative control of most alumni activities. Currently, he believes most campuses desire money without information sharing or policy sharing. He points out that the Internet and social media make communication among alternative alumni voices more feasible now. It takes a lot of time and energy, however, to acquire the information to make an impact. Insisting that accessible campus calendars that record policy relevant debates and lectures be developed and preserved is a first step.

Karen Hyman, Senior Vice President of Policy and Programs at the American Council of Trustees and Alumni, an organization that can play a key role in necessary reform downplays the idea that viewpoint diversity is important. Instead she argues "a return to the liberal arts, the pursuit of truth, the self-critical and self-reflective use of reason and human learning balanced by a sense of the humility about human limits" is the right path.[230] The data show, however, that the humanities fields are among the most ideologically homogeneous and aggressive in their pursuit of politically correct communication. Furthermore, while self-critical and self-reflective use of reason are surely important attributes, preparing students for citizenship requires providing them with substantive information about important contemporary policy issues and experience in the give and take of political debate. Faculty intellectual diversity is the context in which a variety of information and experiences are likely to occur.

Debra Mashek. the new director of the remarkable ad hoc organization of faculty and graduate students—The Heterodox Academy—begins by stating that "Those of us in academia must work to change the campus culture from the bottom up to ensure that there is a free and open exchange of ideas."[231] She supports the development of the concept of "constructive

---

230. A more comprehensive view of ACTA's support for free speech can be found in its April 2018 publication "Building a Culture of Free Expression on the American College Campus." The report written by Joyce Lee Malcom, Patrick Henry Professor of Constitutional Law at George Mason University, criticizes safe spaces, restrictive speech codes, and deplatforming and harassment of speakers, but isn't very explicit about of how a genuine culture of debate could become a regular campus feature.

231. In addition to a website updated weekly, The Heterodox Academy has produced a handsome brochure in 2018 "All Minus One," edited by Richard V. Reeves and Jonathan Haidt about the views of John Stuart Mill on free speech.

disagreement." This "requires a range of cognitive, emotional and social skills, including intellectual humility, curiosity, resilience, respect, perspective taking and empathy." So how do we get there? Mashek says faculty should when curating lists of readings, discussion topics, assignments and guest speakers take care to represent a range of viewpoints. What if they don't for fear of controversy or certitude about their own values?

Then, she argues:

> Campus leadership must be vocal advocates and visible models for constructive disagreement. Sponsor lecture series that explore heterodox ideas. Fund initiatives designed to promote virtuous discourse across constituencies. Include in job ads language that explicitly states viewpoint diversity is welcomed. Hold campus conversations about the values and limits of viewpoint diversity—and soon before your campus experiences a meltdown.

But what if leadership doesn't lead in this regard? With few exceptions, it is not evident it has been doing so. It is inescapable that trustees and legislators must do so, not just after a censorship incident occurs, but to insure that "constructive disagreement" occurs at the institutions on an ongoing basis for which they are responsible. If they must play that role, where will they get the necessary information?

Sean Stevens and Debra Mashek have done research using a sample of 201 Top National Universities and Top National Liberal Arts Colleges as listed in *U S News and World Report*.[232] They found that 17 or 8.46% of these institutions have non-discrimination policies that include political affiliation or political philosophy. The University of Colorado is one of the most forthright "declaring that political affiliation and political philosophy are protected characteristics under the Laws of the Regents." While these general policies may be useful, potential faculty candidates probably pay much more attention to the language in particular job descriptions. Stevens and Mashek describe job ads as:

---

232. Sean Stevens and Debra Mashek, "Non-Discrimination Statements at the Institutional Level & What to Do About It (Part 1)," *The Heterodox Academy* website, November 29, 2017.

carefully crafted to signal institutional needs, interests, and values. Before they are made public, job ads are generally approved by the home department and the academic dean or provost. Some campuses also involve human resource officers and, increasingly, campus diversity officers who weigh in to insure the ad makes clear that the institution welcomes and celebrates diversity.[233]

So of the 17 institutions that have political non-discrimination policies, how were these policies reflected in actual job ads? Only three mentioned non-discrimination based on political affiliation at all and then the phrase was just in the long list of categories the institution affirmed should not be considered in hiring. Only occasionally, such as in the following public policy/ public administration job ad posted by Claremont McKenna Colleges was the concept of intellectual diversity more fleshed out:

> Given our commitment to cultivating a challenging and inclusive educational environment, we seek candidates who can demonstrate a commitment to teaching, mentoring, and inspiring students representing a broad range of socio economic backgrounds, political opinions, genders, race, ethnicities, nationalities, sexual orientations, and religions.[234]

The ideological imbalances on American campuses will not change in any foreseeable future. Universities will rarely define underrepresented groups in political, ideological or religious terms and seek remedies for them as they do for racial, ethnic, and gender groups. External efforts to mandate proportional representation of personnel and ideas would have

---

233. Debra Mashek and Sean Stevens, "Hiring in Higher Ed: Do Job Ads Signal a Desire for Viewpoint Diversity? (Part 2)," *The Heterodox Academy* website, December 1, 2017. See also David Rozado and Stephen Atkins, "Why are Nondiscrimination Statements not Diverse," *Academic Questions*, Fall 2018, Vol 31, No.5 pp. 295–303 which found similar results.

234. Ibid. The authors suggest the following template "We enthusiastically welcome applications from talented individuals from diverse backgrounds. [School Name] values diversity of perspectives, including those held by people from different racial, religious, ideological, ethnic and geographic backgrounds."

undesirable consequences for the value of academic freedom as it should be defined.[235]

Opening up spaces for different ideas, however, can be pursued by sponsoring on-campus debates and forums about important policy issues. That action will send a message to campus groups that when offended they do not have the right to suppress the speech they do not like. Moreover, debates can create recognition and a space for dissenting ideas that will enrich classroom discussions, research agendas, and hiring decisions. **Policy debates can function like tilling exhausted soil so that new life can grow.**

---

235. In 2017, an Iowa State Senator proposed a bill that would require state universities to favor in the hiring process faculty candidates whose political identifications were underrepresented in the hiring department. In an intense on-line discussion in The Heterodox Academy website, whose members are interested in increasing intellectual diversity in higher education, there was very little support for using legislation to achieve it. Jonathan Haidt, "Iowa State Senator Proposes Misguided Diversity Bill," February 25, 2017. http://heterodoxacadmy.org/2017/02/25/iowa-misguided-diversity-bill.

Chapter III.
Creating and Committing to a
Culture of Debate

In recent years on too many campuses, the stages on which a vigorous healthy political discourse should take place have gone silent. Speakers have been disinvited or heckled into silence; newspapers stolen or posters ripped down: and most frequently debates or forums with diverse viewpoints on controversial subjects are just not scheduled. Avoidance seems the safest path. Several new books emerged to make the case in philosophical and practical terms for academic freedom.[236] These books may incentivize some faculty and administrators to buttress the rules against these disruptions, particularly in light of disastrous aftermath of problems at Missouri and Evergreen.

More often, however, faculty and staff may just slap themselves on the back in self-congratulation that such disruptions have not occurred at their institutions; believing, therefore, their campus freedom of speech is heathy. But silence is not a sign of academic health or freedom, particularly if one segment of political opinion on campus feels intimidated to speak out, as some surveys suggest (Brookings, CATO, and The Heterodox Academy).[237] As welcome as these books are, they do not provide many suggestions for creating room on campuses for the dissenting ideas that exist in the larger

---

236. Keith Whittington, *Speak Freely: Why Universities Must Defend Free Speech*, (Princeton: Princeton University Press 2018), Nadine Strossen, *HATE: Why We Should Resist It with Free Speech, Not Censorship* (New York: Oxford University Press, 2018), Greg Lukianoff and Jonathan Haidt, *The Coddling of the American Mind: How Good Intentions and Bad Ideas are Setting Up a Generation for Failure* (New York: Penguin Press, 2018).

237. See references to these studies in footnotes 213, 214, and 216.

society and that student should hear to prepare themselves for engaged citizenship. For that to happen, students must be encouraged to move beyond their ideological silos, and those of their faculty, to hear policy debates by speakers who know the issues and respectfully disagree with each other on some points.

When students, with considerable faculty support, at Middlebury, disrupted a 2017 speech by Charles Murray, it is fair to ask how well their education had prepared them to hear ideas with which they were predisposed not to like. According to its 2014 and 2015 College calendars, this top ten liberal arts campus with 2,526 students supported by an endowment of a billion dollars sponsored no policy debates, only one forum with divergent policy viewpoints, and four forums with uncertain viewpoint diversity. Should the Middlebury administration have been shocked at the campus reaction to Murray? Or was it complicit in creating the ideological homogeneity students heard every day on campus?

What can be done to create a campus culture of civil debate, to unlock the stages where political discourse should take place?[238] Reforms must meet the test of scalability, compatibility, and accountability. There are more than 3,000 institutions of higher education in the United States. As valuable as institutes and organizations promoting free speech and debates may be on the few campuses that have them, they have only local impact and survive only as long as their faculty sponsors and funders remain engaged. There is no sign that higher education sees them as models that should be adopted on any wide spread basis.

Proposals that challenge the one-sided politicization of contemporary American higher education need to be heard and seem to be having some impact on public opinion. Changing institutional priorities and structures is very difficult, however, if the critics are seen simply as opponents of the establishment. The increasing corporatization of universities is unlikely to be reversed. The tendency of administrators to defer and even fund campus political identity groups that seek to control permissible speech will be

---

238. A thoughtful overview of campus free speech issues can be found in the 2016 report by PEN titled "And Campus for All: Diversity, Inclusion and Freedom of Speech in U.S. Universities" and "PEN America Principles on Campus Free Speech" PEN which is devoted to protecting free speech for writers provides a well-balanced perspective of the issues and offers some useful, if very general suggestions, on how to handle various conflicts. The reports are not very helpful, however, in describing a pro-active campus agenda for embracing the necessary debates on which democracy depends.

perpetuated given the influence of those groups in the personnel process. The ideological composition of the faculty will not change in any foreseeable future. Reform must speak to values that higher education regards as compatible with its truth-seeking mission.

What is possible is to urge that free speech and political discourse on campuses be expanded and protected. Even at an institution that never actually sponsors on-campus debates open to all, administrators and faculty will not admit they are opposed to that concept. They just never get around to actually hosting them. There are some well-known educators who are vigorous in their defense of dialogue and debate. Many have been previously cited in this research. For example, Mark Yudof, President Emeritus of the University of California, has written:

> The fact is that, despite the hallowed traditions of academic freedom and freedom of inquiry, many campuses are hostile to genuine conversation and debate. Freedom of expression is viewed by a vocal minority as a ploy to preserve privilege. There is a fear of even listening to those with whom one disagrees. Campuses are viewed as "safe" only if they are ideologically pure.[239]

There are, however, organizational allies with national constituencies for free speech. Both the American Council of Education and the Association of Governing Boards have made general statements supporting intellectual diversity. Other organizations such as the American Council of Trustees and Alumni, the Federalist Society, the Foundation for Individual Rights in Education, The Heterodox Academy, the James G. Martin Center, and the National Association of Scholars have been more focused and energetic in their efforts to defend freedom of speech and intellectual diversity. Perhaps one day, even the American Association of University Professors and the American Civil Liberties Union will return regularly to the campus free speech battles they fought before.[240] When speakers, newspapers, and debates are shut down, all these allies have a stake in promoting openness.

---

239. "Colleges should commit to robust debates about Middle East conflicts," *Inside Higher Education,* December 14, 2015.

240. The AAUP has vigorously defended individual faculty who have been threatened for their speech, often on social media, but has not similarly been concerned with campus incidents which threatened speech for the whole academic community. The ACLU has decided to focus its energies elsewhere than classic free speech issues.

Nationally, campuses need to evaluate whether they have a culture of ideological conformity, and if so, move to a culture of policy debate. There needs to be leadership and accountability for achieving that goal on every campus.

A. Trustee and Legislative Accountability

In the modern era, campuses are accountable to a wide variety of institutions for a breathtaking number of issues. How to hold them accountable for intellectual diversity, however, has been little explored. Whenever a campus makes reports on "diversity" by race, ethnicity and gender, it ought to show how it has identified intellectual diversity and measured it. By far the best approach is for traditional campus governance (trustees, administrators, faculty senates, and student organizations) to take that responsibility. Accrediting bodies and state governments might play a secondary role, particularly if a campus has affirmed a responsibility for intellectual diversity and has sought funding premised on that purpose, but has no demonstrable evidence that it has made any progress in achieving that goal. In the worst case scenario, a campus that tolerates disinvited or heckled speakers, stolen newspapers or other forms of speech suppression might be subject to sanctions. Such patterns suggest that academic freedom is not taught or valued on that campus and that students are being deprived of the richness of intellectual diversity available in the larger American culture.

The place to begin for any accountability reviews is to examine the number and variety of on-campus debates and open forums with participants who express divergent views. **Campuses with a rich culture of debate will often suffer less from a culture of intellectual conformity that may lead some community members to believe they should suppress speech and cause other members of the community to remain silent.**

Trustees and state legislators customarily obtain and evaluate the fiscal balance sheets of the campuses for which they are responsible, but rarely examine their intellectual balance sheets. They can, however play an important role by simply asking questions and insisting on answers and annual reports to support those answers. The key questions are:

1. Does your campus include among its missions, citizenship preparation that exposes students to diverse viewpoints regarding major policy issues?

2. Does your campus have a publicly accessible electronic calendar covering recent years, so that the campus intellectual history related to public policy debates, forums or lectures can be examined? If not, why not?[241]

3. How many policy debates or policy forums with divergent viewpoints open to all students took place on your campus in the last five years? Who were the sponsors, participants, and topics of those policy events?

4. Is there any administrative office or faculty body responsible for seeing that a balanced presentation of policy events with diverse viewpoints takes place each year on your campus?

5. Are there any policy issues widely debated in the public at large that you think would be inappropriate to be debated on your campus?[242]

In February 2017, Stanley Kurtz, James Manley, and Jonathan Butcher released a report, "Campus Free Speech: A Legislative Proposal" under the auspices of the Goldwater Institute. Earlier the Institute convinced the Arizona legislature to enact a prohibition against campus safe speech zones that otherwise restricted free speech.[243] Their new legislative proposal is much more comprehensive and includes these elements as model law for any state university: (1) requiring an official policy encouraging free speech; (2) preventing administrators from disinviting controversial speakers; (3) creating a system of disciplinary sanctions for students or others who interfere with campus speech; (4) creating due process procedures for

---

241. See footnote 119 and the surrounding discussion. Campuses which keep meticulous records of their athletic events are very erratic in their recording of campus wide intellectual events. Unlike for athletics, no one is charged with that that academic task.

242. George R. La Noue, "Promoting a Campus Culture of Policy Debates." *Academic Questions*. Winter, 2017. Vol.30, No, 4.

243. In addition to Arizona, Missouri, Tennessee, and Virginia have passed legislation restricting the use of free speech zones. New Hampshire, Washington, Texas, Kentucky, North Dakota, Colorado and Utah were considering such legislation in 2017. *Politico Morning Education*. March 17, 2017. Peter Schmidt, "Tennessee Law is hailed as Offering Unprecedented Protection of Campus Speech," *The Chronicle of Higher Education*, June 6, 2017. See also, Colleen Flaherty, "Critics of Proposed Legislation on First Amendment rights at Wisconsin public universities say it goes too far," *Inside Higher Education*, May 15, 2017. See also, Jeremy W. Peters, "In Name of Free Speech, a Crackdown on Campus Protests," *New York Times,* June 18, 2018.

those accused of interfering with free speech; (5) allowing persons whose speech has been infringed to seek the recovery of court costs and attorney fees; (6) reaffirming that institutions should be neutral on public policy issues; and (7) requiring institutional boards to create "subcommittees to issue yearly reports to the public, the trustees, the governor, and the legislature on the administrative handling of free speech." The Goldwater Institute team noted that "An annual report on the administrative handling of these issues will either hold the president accountable or be subject to public criticism for failing to do so."[244]

The 2018 North Carolina Campus Free Speech Act is the first in the country to require university trustees to issue an annual public report on the condition of free speech among public campuses.[245] Before the Act was passed, however, the provision requiring institutions to strive toward neutrality on political issues was struck out. Kurtz concedes that campuses cannot be completely politically neutral, for example, on issues that directly affect them such as state funding, but on non-educational issues he contends that should be the goal because: "If the university, as an institution, were to take an official position on a controversial issue like the role of government in healthcare or American foreign policy in the Middle East, that would put pressure on individual faculty and students to toe the official university line."[246] The Act does require campuses to report on . . . "substantial difficulties, controversies or successes in maintaining a posture of administrative and institutional neutrality with regard to political and social issues."

The Kurtz et.al. recommendation for required campus reporting on free speech is quite compatible with the questions for legislators and trustees this book suggests with this important difference.[247] The Goldwater pro-

---

244. Stanley Kurtz, James Manley and Jonathan Butcher, "Campus Free Speech: A Legislative Proposal" (Phoenix Az.: The Goldwater Institute, 2017). For another view of implementing protections of free speech and academic freedom on campus, see Althea Nagai, "Going Beyond Proclamation: Implementing Free Speech Principles," *Academic Questions*, Winter 2017, Vol. 30. No. 4.

245. Stanley Kurtz, "Implementing the North Carolina Campus Free Speech Act," The James G. Martin Center, May 28, 2018.

246. The historical articulation of this position is in the 1967 University of Chicago Kalven Commission Report.

247. Magdalene Horzempa, "Free Speech at UNC: Improvement, but Still Lots to Do," James G. Martin Center, August 27, 2018. This article evaluates the system's compliance with the Act and generally finds that campuses avoided incidents damaging to free speech,

posal seeks to remove roadblocks to campus free speech, while this book challenges administrators to assure that a highway is built that will improve campus political discourse and intellectual diversity. Surely, one of the best ways to insure institutional neutrality on controversial political and social issues is to sponsor debates about them, instead of relying solely on protests, manifestos or dictates to reflect varying opinions. **Without both approaches, clearing away the barriers to free speech and a positive affirmation of a culture of debate, the goal of educating students for their full citizen responsibilities will not be achieved.**

B. Faculty and External Funding

The major barrier to hosting on-campus policy debates, in most cases, is not their cost.[248] Few, if any, campuses spend more on public policy debates than on even their most minor varsity sports. It is usually a matter of institutional priorities, not money. If it is part of an institutional ethos and well-organized, faculty and alumni should be willing to participate without further compensation. Nevertheless, in academia, funding can always trigger energy and innovation. Faculty can play a key role in initiating grant requests for policy debates or forums, if institutions are supportive and regard such activities as part of faculty service responsibilities. Some funders, such as governments[249] or some foundations prefer broad based funding, but other funders will prefer to be more targeted.

Perhaps the outstanding example of targeted debate funding is the Arthur N. Rupe Foundation. It sponsors "debates that advance civil and reasoned public debate at the high school, university and civic level." These debates are:

> non-partisan and accessible to a general audience, with the intention of educating and exposing audiences to all sides of a particular social issue. It is the foundation's hope to increase the number of Americans

---

except for the use of a "bias response" team at UNC Ashville. With regard to political neutrality, the evaluation faulted the selection of summer reading books.

248. Campuses often have budget line items for lecture series, often endowed, but we did not discover any such budget set asides for policy debates.

249. The requirement in some federal programs that a share of the funding go to civic engagement could easily encompass a program of policy debates.

actively in debates, as it forms the cornerstone of an informed elector-
ate in a free society.[250]

To implement that goal, the foundation has funded a series of annual debates at the University of California Santa Barbara[251] and the Benjamin
Rush debates at medical schools across the country.[252]

Funding for even broader campus dialogues on public policy has recently been provided to Johns Hopkins University by the Stavros Niarchos
Foundation in a $150 million gift. The money will be used to recreate the
concept of the Athenian Agora which created a common space for people
to coexist as citizens to engage in political discourse and the exchange of
ideas.[253]

If a campus believes it has a documented a general intellectual diversity
problem, it could seek funding to correct that deficiency. Sometimes major
institutional efforts and funding will be required as it has been for other
diversity efforts. Sometimes smaller amounts used for lectures, debates or
visiting or adjunct faculty will make a difference. If a campus is perceived
as having no interest in intellectual diversity, it should not be surprised
if some state legislators or private funders do not respond warmly when
asked to support existing intellectual conformity.[254]

---

250. http://www.rupefoundation.org/ (accessed 1/11/2017).

251. In 2014–15, "The Use of Genetically Modified Food, 2012–2013, "Drone Warfare:
Prospects and Dangers" and 2011–2012 "Academic Freedom in a time of Crisis."

252. In 2016, these debates "Government healthcare v. the free-market" (Ohio State);
"Free market v. Government-Run Healthcare" (George Washington University); "Is 'Colorado Care' right for Colorado?" (University of Colorado Boulder); and "What is the Government's Role in Health Care?" (SUNY Stony Brook).

253. Tim Prudente, "Hopkins gets grant for civil discourse," *Baltimore Sun,* June 23,
2017. The Agora Institute will be housed in a new building and will be staffed by 10 professors with interdisciplinary backgrounds.

254. There has been a long term controversy about whether the federal government's
funding of Middle Eastern Studies programs which were created out of national security
concerns have reflected viewpoint balances. The Louis Brandeis D. Center "The Morass of
Middle East Studies: Title VI of the Higher Education Act and Federally Funded Areas Studies, 2014. In its 2008 reauthorization, Congress required programs to provide "diverse perspectives" and "wide range of views to generate debate on world regions and international
affairs." Implementation by the Department of Education was lax, however. pp. 16–18. The
Brandeis Center recommended funding applicants demonstrate (1) positive learning outcomes, (2) establishment of a critical mass of diverse viewpoints related to substantive perspectives and (3) protect academic freedom by not encroaching on curriculum decisions or
classroom instruction. p 34.

The campus responsibility is to sponsor and publicize policy debates and forums with divergent viewpoints; it need not produce all the substantive content itself. While sometimes a debate focusing on historical issues may be useful, the most productive debates for informing citizenship decisions will feature dialogues within the framework of contemporary issues. For example a debate on foreign policy regarding Iran or North Korea or domestic issues such as health or immigration policy would be very different in the fall of 2018 than it would have been five years ago. Many campuses will not have the internal resources to conduct such a debate. For that reason, research centers, think tanks and other sources could use their expertise to produce and stockpile on the Internet policy debates in their specialties for any campus to show. When external events dictated, these debates could be updated.

C. Students and Families

Even, if the accountability and production problems can be solved, policy debates are not on most students' radars. Families need to play a role in creating demand. Many Americans are very concerned about the intensely polarized nature of our contemporary political discourse. Students may not have much perspective on those matters and may retreat to late night shows for information and which at least purport to be humorous

Except for the very most selective campuses, there will be a buyer's market for admissions for the foreseeable future. Families shop campuses carefully considering financial aid, career prospects, campus safety and environment, housing and food options, recreation, athletic, and cultural activities. Students who are being vigorously recruited will be treated to specially designed efforts to assure them their interests will be nurtured and that appropriate role models exist. Statistics on the race, ethnicity, and gender of faculty and students will be readily available.

Campuses do not publicly admit that they take no responsibility to educate their students about important public policy issues, even if they may not have any programs to promote those goals. What if students interested in a variety of public affairs issues have to turn to off-campus sources such as the electronic or press news media where there is little opportunity to question editorial decisions or the bias of speakers? What if the campus is one where in a number of the most politically relevant departments, there is only ideological conformity on policy issues? It would take some effort for families or external stakeholders to get answers to these questions, but it could be done.

The first obvious question, because the answer should be clear-cut, for concerned families and students is does this school sponsor on-campus policy debates; and, if so, on what topics and with which participants? If there are few or no such campus debates, ask why not? Ask if there are other open forums in which students can hears divergent viewpoints about issues on which they will soon be voting? An answer that suggests that neither administrators, faculty, nor the current students would regard such events as worthwhile enough to organize should set off alarm bells.

On a more personal level, if the prospective student knows what he or she will likely major in or what kind of career will be pursued, then families can ask whether mentors with diverse viewpoints will be available to guide independent studies or internships and write recommendations. A list of recent internships will probably be available. If a student wants to explore a particular ideological or religious perspective, but no faculty will provide guidance in that area, that could be a powerful disincentive for the student to grow in his or her intellectual interests.

In short, families concerned about intellectual diversity in the college experience need to ask the right questions and to write follow-up comments if the answers are vague or misleading. Disgruntled or concerned consumers will attract attention in today's admissions' marketplace.

A public inventory of campus debates and open forums, as this research has done, should be the first step in holding higher education accountable for exposing students and future citizens to diverse ideas. That should eventually improve to the kind of civil and tolerant political culture so important in a democracy. As President John F. Kennedy once declared "Without debate, without criticism, no Administration and no country can succeed—and no republic can survive."[255] There is plenty of criticism in American politics currently, much of it loud and intemperate. What is lacking are policy debates focused on constructive engagement that is informed and respectful of viewpoint differences. Higher education is the best place to train for those kind of debates and to create audiences that believe that such are essential in a democracy.

---

255. John F Kennedy "Address to the American Newspapers Publishers Association," April 27, 1961.

Bibliography

Books and Reports

American Association of Colleges and Universities, *A Crucible Moment: College Learning and Democracy's Future.* 2012.

American Association of University Professors, *The History, Uses, and Abuses of Title IX.* 2016.

American Council on Education, "Statement of Academic Rights and Responsibilities," June, 2005.

American Council of Trustees and Alumni, "Intellectual Diversity: Time for Action." December 2005.

American Council of Trustees and Alumni, "Protecting the Free Exchange of Ideas: How Trustees Can Advance Intellectual Diversity on Campus," 2009.

American Council of Trustees and Alumni, "No U.S. History?," July 2016.

Ash, Timothy Garton, *Free Speech: Ten Principles for a Connected World.* New Haven: Yale University Press, 2016.

Baker, C. Edwin and Nicholas F. Galliocchio, *Human Liberty and Freedom of Speech.* New York: Oxford University Press.1989.

Ben-Porath, Sigal, *Free Speech on Campus.* Philadelphia: University of Pennsylvania Press, 2017.

Berman, Paul, ed. *Debating P.C. The Controversy over Political Correctness on College Campuses.* New York: Dell Publishing, 1992.

Bernstein, Richard, *The Dictatorship of Virtue.* New York: Alfred A. Knopf, 1994.

Bilgammi, Akeel, (eds.) and Jonathan R. Cole (eds.). *Who's Afraid of Academic Freedom.* New York: Columbia University Press, 2015.

Bloom, Alan, *Closing of the American Mind.* New York: Simon and Schuster, 1987.

Bok, Derek, *Universities in the Marketplace: The Commercialization of Higher Education.* Princeton: Princeton University Press, 2003.

Bowen, Catherine Drinker, *Miracle at Philadelphia*. Boston: Little, Brown and Company, 1985.

Bowen, Howard R. and Jack H. Schuster, *American Professors: A Natural Resource Imperiled*. New York: Oxford University Press, 1986.

Brown University Speakers Report: "Monitoring Our School's Commitment to Diversity of Thought," 2017.

Chamberlin, Pam, "Deliberate Differences: Progressive and Conservative Activism in the United States Campuses," Political Research Association, 2012.

Chemerinsky, Erwin and Howard Gillian, Free *Speech on Campus* New Haven, Ct.: Yale University Press, 2016.

Downs, Donald Alexander, *Restoring Free Speech and Liberty on Campuses*. Oakland, Ca.: The Independent Institute, 2005.

Durate, Jose L. et.al. "Political Diversity Will Improve Social Psychological Science," *Behavioral and Brain Sciences*. Cambridge University Press, 2014.

Ellis, Joseph J., *The Quartet*. New York: Alfred A. Knopf, 2015.

Evergreen College, "Report of The Independent External Review Panel on the Evergreen College Response to the Spring 2017 campus events."

Ford, Paul L. ed., *The Writings of Thomas Jefferson*. Vol. 10. New York: Cosimo Classics, 2010.

Freedom Forum Institute, "The 2018 State of the First Amendment."

Gallup, Inc., "Free Expression on Campus: A Survey of U.S. College Students and U.S. Adults," September 23, 2016.

Gates, Henry, Jr. ed. *"Speaking of Race; Speaking of Sex; Hate Speech, Civil Rights and Civil Liberties*. New York: New York University Press, 1994.

Ginsberg, Benjamin, *The Fall of the Faculty: The Rise of the All-Administrative University and Why it Matters*. New York: Oxford University Press, 2011.

Guelzo, Allen C., *Lincoln and Douglas: The Debates that Defined America*. New York: Simon and Schuster, 2008.

Ham, Mary Katherine and Guy Benson, *End of Discussion, How the Left's Outrage Industry Shuts Down Debate*. New York: Crown Forum, 2015.

Hamilton, Alexander, James Madison, and John Jay, *The Federalist Papers*, ed. Jim Miller. Mineola, N.Y.: Dover Publications, 2014.

Herbst, Susan, *Rude Democracy: Civility and Incivility in American Politics*. Philadelphia: Temple University Press, 2010.

Hofstadter, Richard Hofstadter, *Academic Freedom in the Age of the College*. Piscataway, N.J.: Transaction Press, reprinted 1995.

Jaffa, Harry K., *Crisis of a House Divided: An Interpretation of the Lincoln-Douglas Debates Fiftieth Anniversary Edition*. Chicago: University of Chicago Press, 2009.

Johnson, K.J. and Stuart Taylor Jr., *The Campus Rape Frenzy: The Attack on Due Process at America's Universities*. New York: Encounter Books, 2017.

Knox, Emily J. M., (ed.) *Trigger Warnings: History, Theory and Context*. Lanham, MD: Rowman & Littlefield, 2017.

Kurtz, Stanley James Manley and Jonathan Butcher, "Campus Free Speech: A Legislative Proposal." Phoenix Az.: The Goldwater Institute, 2017.

Lee, Philip, *Academic Freedom and American Universities*. Lanham, MD.: Lexington Books, 2016.

Lencioni, Patrick, *The Five Dysfunctions of a Team*. San Francisco: Jossey Bass, 2002.

Lukianoff, Greg, *Unlearning Liberty, Campus Censorship and the End of American Debate*. New York: Encounter Books, 2012.

Lukianoff, Greg and Jonathan Haidt, *The Coddling of the American Mind: How Good Intentions and Bad Ideas are Setting Up a Generation for Failure*. New York: Penguin Press, 2018.

Malcolm, Joyce Lee, *Building a Culture of Free Expression on the American College Campus*, American Council of Trustees and Alumni, April 2018.

Marcus, Lawrence R., *Fighting Words: The Politics of Hate Speech*. New York: Praeger, 1996.

Metzger, Walter P., *Academic Freedom in the Age of the University*. New York: Columbia University Press, 1961.

Myers, Jeremy, Bruce L.R. Smith and A. Lee Fritschler, *Closed Minds? Politics and Ideology in American Universities*. Washington, D.C. The Brookings Institution, 2008.

PEN "And Campus for All: Diversity, Inclusion and Freedom of Speech in U.S. Universities" 2016 PEN American Principles on Campus Free Speech".

Pew Research Center, "Political Polarization in the American Public," June 12, 2014

Powers, Kristen, *The Silencing: How the Left is Killing Free Speech*. Washington, D.C: Regnery Publishing, 2015.

Randall, David, *Making Citizens: How American Universities Teach Civics*. New York: National Association of Scholars, 2017.

Robinson, Randy, *Free Speech on America's K-12 and College Campuses*. Lanham, MD: Lexington Books, 2016.

Schrecker, Ellen The *Lost Soul of Higher Education: Corporatization, the Assault on Academic Freedom and the End of the American University*. New York: The New Press, 2010.

Senate, U. S., Health, Education and Labor Committee, "Recalibrating Regulation of Colleges and Universities," http:/www.help.senate.gov/imo/media/Regulations_Task_Force_Report_2015_FINAL.pdf.

Shields Jon A. and Joshua M. Dunn Sr., *Passing on the Right: Conservative Professors in the Progressive University*. New York: Oxford University Press, 2016.

Shiffrin, Steven H., *What's Wrong with the First Amendment*. Cambridge: Cambridge University Press, 2016.

Strossen, Nadine, *HATE: Why We Should Resist It with Free Speech, Not Censorship*. New York: Oxford University Press, 2018.

Sykes, Charles J., *Fail U. The False Promise of Higher Education*. New York: St. Martin's Press, 2016.

Volokh, Eugene, *The First Amendment*. New York: Foundation Press, 2013.

Walker, Samuel, *Hate Speech: The History of an American Controversy*. Lincoln, NE: University of Nebraska Press, 1994.

Washburn, Jennifer, *University, Inc.: The Corporate Corruption of Higher Education*. New York: Basic Books, 2005.

Whittington, Keith *Speak Freely: Why Universities Must Defend Free Speech*. Princeton: Princeton University Press, 2018.

Williams, Joanna, *Academic Freedom in an Age of Conformity*. Basingstoke, U.K.: Palgrave McMillan, 2016.

Wood, Zachery R., *Uncensored: My Life and Uncomfortable Conversations at the Intersection of Black and White America*. New York: Dutton, 2018.

Articles

Abrams, Sam. "The Blue Shift of the New England Professoriate," *The Heterodox Academy* website, July 6, 2016.

Abrams, Samuel J, "Many students embrace viewpoint diversity. Why Won't Colleges?" *Real Clear Education*, https://realcleareducation.com/articles/2017/12/15/many-students.

Abrams, Samuel, "Think Professors Are Liberal? Try College Administrators," *New York Times*, October 16, 2018.

Adams, Mike and Adam Kissel, "Censorship in the UNC System: Correcting the Narrative," *Academic Questions*, Summer 2017, Vol. 30, No.2. Abrams, Samuel J, "There are Conservative Professors, Just not in These States," *New York Times Sunday Review*, July 1, 2016.

Alcabes, Phillip, "Our Idea of Tolerant Isn't," *The Chronicle of Higher Education*, October 21, 2016.

American Council of Trustees and Alumni, "Better Angels Counters Polarization on Campus," Vol. XXIII, No.4, 2017–2018.

"An Open Letter to the Wesleyan Community from Students of Color." Posted at: wesleying.org/2015/09/25.

Bass, Scott A. and Mary L. Clark, "The Gravest Threat to Colleges Comes From Within," *The Chronicle for Higher Education,* September 28, 2015.

Bauerlein, Marc, "A Very Long Disengagement," *The Chronicle of Higher Education*, January 6, 2006.

Bauer-Wolf, Jeremy, "William & Mary students who shut down ACLU event broke student code," *Inside Higher Education*, October 6, 2017.

Bauer-Wolf, Jeremy "New student coalition alleges press is suppressed at Christian institutions," *Inside Higher Education*, May 23, 2018.

Bauer-Wolf, Jeremy "Civility at Berkeley," *Inside Higher Education,* November 28, 2018.

"Blue on blue," *The Economist,* September 9, 2017,

Brown, Sarah, "Should a Syllabus Ever Tell Students What Not to Say?" *The Chronicle for Higher Education,* October 8, 2015.

Brown, Sarah and Katherine Mangan, "What 'Safe Spaces' Really Look Like on College Campuses," *The Chronicle of Higher Education,* September 16. 2016.

Brown, Sarah "At Yale, Painful Rifts Emerge Over Diversity and Free Speech," *The Chronicle of Higher Education,* October, 2016.

Burleigh, Nina, "The Battle Against 'Hate Speech' on College Campuses Gives Rise to a Generation that Hates Speech," *Newsweek,* May 26, 2016.

Carl, Noah "New Report on the Political Views of the British Academics," *The Heterodox Academy* website. March 6, 2017.

Carle, Robert, "The Strange Career of Title IX," *Academic Questions*, Winter 2016, Vol. 29, No.4.

Carlson, Scott, "Spending Shifts as Colleges Compete on Students' Comfort," *The Chronicle of Higher Education,* July 28. 2014.

Chemerinsky, Erwin, and Howard Gillman, "Free speech, Rebalanced," *The Chronicle of Higher Education*, April 15, 2016.

Christakis, Nicholas "Teaching Inclusion in a Divided World," *New York Tines,* June 22, 2016.

Cogan, Marin "The Twilight of Free Speech Liberalism," *The New Republic*, July 16, 2018.

"College Presidents see disconnect with public, worry about Washington," *Inside Higher Education*, March 10, 2017.

Deruy, Emily, "The Fine Line Between Safe Space and Segregation," *The Atlantic*, August 2016.

Drezner, Daniel W. "The trouble with 21st Century campus politics," *The Washington Post*, November 9, 2015.

Ekins, Emily, "20% of College Students say College Faculty Has Balanced Mix of Political Views," November 6, 2017. https://www.cato.org/blog/20-current -students-say-college-faculty-has-balanced-mix-political-views.

Etchemendy, John, "The Threat from Within," *The Chronicle of Higher Education*, March 17, 2017.

Faust, Drew Gilpin, "The University's Crisis of Purpose," *The New York Times Book Review,* September 6, 2009.

Flaherty, Colleen "Critics of Proposed Legislation on First Amendment rights at Wisconsin public universities say it goes too far," *Inside Higher Education*, May 15, 2017.

Flaherty, Colleen, "Knox College calls off Brecht play after complaints of racial insensitivity," *Inside Higher Education*, November 10, 2017.

Flaherty, Colleen, "Divided Wisconsin Supreme Court Backs Marquette Faculty Blogger," *Inside Higher Education,* July 9, 2018. *John McAdams v. Marquette University*, July 6, 2018.

F.I.R.E. "One Man's Vulgarity: Art censorship on American Campuses," 2018.

Foster, Ben, "Disconnect: Kentucky and the Political Ideology of its Public Universities," *Academic Questions*, Fall 2018. Vol 31, No.4 pp.313–312.

Friedersdorf, Connor, "The Perils of Writing a Provocative Email at Yale, "*The Atlantic*, May 26, 2016.

George, Robert P., "Why Academic Freedom Matters (Now More Than Ever)," *Intercollegiate Review* Online, June 18, 2018.

Gillman, Ollie, "The Moment Yale Students Encircled and Shouted Down Professor Who Told Them to Just 'Look Away' if They Were Offended by Halloween Customs," *Daily Mail,* November 7, 2015.

Gitlin, Todd, "Reason's Last Stand," *The Chronicle of Higher Education*, March 17, 2017. Stanford News, "Stanford launched Cardinal Conversations initiative to expose campus to diverse views," January 10, 2018.

Golash-Boza, Tanya, "How to Write an Effective Diversity Statement," *Inside Higher Education*, June 10, 2016, https://www.insidehighered.com/advice/2016/06/10/how-write-effective-diversity-statement-essay.

Goldberg, Suzanne B., "Free Expression on Campus: Mitigating the Cost of Contentious Speakers," *Harvard Journal of Law & Public Policy,* Vol. 41, No 1, (Winter, 2018).

Green, Erica L., "Education Depart Reopens Rutgers Case Charging Discrimination Against Jewish Students," *New York Times*, September 11, 2018.

Grinberg, Raffi, "Lindsey Shepard and the Potential for Heterodoxy at Wilfrid Laurier University," *The Heterodox Academy* website, November, 23, 2017.

Grossman, Matt. and David A. Hopkins, "How the conservative movement has undermined trust in higher education," *Inside Higher Education*," October 11, 2016.

Haidt, Jonathan, "Iowa State Senator Proposes Misguided Diversity Bill," February 25, 2017. http://heterodoxacadmy.org/2017/02/25/iowa-misguided-diversity-bill.

Hartocollis, Anemona, "College Student Protest, Alumni Fondness Fades and Checks Shrink," *The New York Times,* August 5, 2016.

Harris, Uri, "How Activists Took Control of a University: The Case Study of Evergreen State," *Quillette*, December 22, 2017.

Harvard Law Faculty, "Rethink Harvard's Sexual Harassment Policy," *Boston Globe*, October 15, 2015.

Hendershott, Anne, "Are Alumni Pulling the Policy in Academia?" *Minding The Campus,* June 11, 2018.

Henning, Anthony, "Colleges Reject the Duty to Teach Liberty's Framework," The James G. Martin Center, July 4, 2018.

Hess, Frederick M., "Lukewarm Column on 'Black lives matter' sparks demand for reeducation," *National Review,* September 23, 2015.

Hess, Frederick M. and Grant Addison, "Restoring Free Inquiry on Campus," *National Affairs,* Spring, 2018.

Hoover, Eric, "The Comfortable Kid," *The Chronicle of Higher Education,* July 28, 2014.

Horowitz, Mark, Anthony L. Haynor, and Kenneth Kickham, "Sociology's Sacred Victims and the Politics of Knowledge: Moral Foundations Theory and Disciplinary Controversies," *The American Sociologist,* June *2018.*

Horzempa, Magdalene, "Free Speech at UNC: Improvement, but Still Lots to Do," James G. Martin Center, August 27 2018.

Hudson, Matthew, "Why Liberals Aren't as Tolerant as They Think," *Politico,* May 9, 2017.

Jackson, Sarah and Victor Porcelli. "Henry Kissinger Told to 'Rot in Hell.' Disrupted Four Times During Talk at Stern," October 16, 2018. news@nyu.com.

Jaschik, Scott, *"Protest Over Bishop Tutu as Speaker at Gonzaga," Inside Higher Education*, April 12, 2012.

Jaschik, Scott, "Free Speech at Brown (Again)," *Inside Higher Education,* November 7, 2013.

Jaschik, Scott, "Harvard Debates Bloomberg as Commencement Speaker," *Inside Higher Education*, March 14, 2014.

Jaschik, Scott, "Yale professors issue an open letter on free speech," *Inside Higher Education*, December 1, 2015.

Jaschik, Scott, "Academic at center of Yale controversy over Halloween costumes won't teach there again," *Inside Higher Education,* December 7, 2015.

Jaschik, Scott, "U British Columbia Restores Invitation to Speaker," *Inside Higher Education*, January 10, 2016.

Jaschik, Scott, "U of Chicago warns incoming students not to expect safe spaces or trigger warnings," *Inside Higher Education*, August 25, 2016.

Jaschik, Scott, "Professors and Politics: What the Research Says," *Inside Higher Education*, February 27, 2017.

Jaschik, Scott, "Middlebury students shout down lecture by Charles Murray," March 3, 2017.

Jaschik, Scott, "Middlebury engages in soul-searching after speech is shouted down and professor is attacked." March 6, 2017.

Jaschik, Scott, "Middlebury president vows 'accountability' for those who disrupted lecture and attacked professor," *Inside Higher Education*. March 7, 2017.

Jaschik, Scott, "College Presidents see disconnect with public. . . " *Inside Higher Education*, March 10, 2017.

Jaschik, Scott, "Middlebury announces additional punishments related to disruption of Charles Murray lecture," *Inside Higher Education*, May 15, 2017.

Jaschik, Scott, "Claremont McKenna suspends 5 students for blocking a speech," *Inside Higher Education*, July 18, 2017.

Jaschik, Scott, "Study suggests it's not just students who have difficulty understanding free expression," *Inside Higher Education,* November 10, 2017.

Jaschik, Scott, "Britain May Fine Universities That Limit Free Speech," *Inside Higher Education*, January 2, 2018.

Jaschik, Scott, "Justice Dept. Backs Suit Against Berkeley, *Inside Higher Education,* January 26, 2018.

Jaschik, Scott, "Students interrupt several portions of speech by Christina Hoff Sommers," *Inside Higher Education*. March 6, 2018.

Jaschik, Scott, "Guest lecture on free speech at CUNY law school heckled," *Inside Higher Education*, April 16, 2018.

Jaschik, Scott, "Falling Confidence in Higher Ed," *Inside Higher Education,* October 9, 2018.

Johnson, K.C., "Safe Spaces and Defending the Academic Status Quo," *Academic Questions,* Spring 2017, Vol. 30, No. 1.

Johnson, K.C., "Janus and the Campus," *City Journal*, July 1, 2018.

Joyce, Phillip, "How Academia is Failing Government: Because the incentives for academic research are misaligned, it has little impact on the real world of public administration and policy." *Governing.* August 31, 2016.

Kaminer, Wendy, "The progressive ideas behind the lack of free speech on campus," *The Washington Post*, February 20, 2015.

Kaminer, Wendy, "The ACLU Retreats From Free Expression," *The Wall Street Journal*, June 20, 2018.

Kellerman, Eric, "Mizzou tries to heal its fractured relationship with Its Legislature," *The Chronicle for Higher Education*, March 4, 2016.

Kirchik, Jamie, "Reflections on the Revolution at Yale," *Quillette*, September 9, 2018.

Kerns, Madeleine, "Viewpoint Diversity Dies at Sarah Lawrence College," *National Review*, November 6, 2018.

Kimbrough, Walter, "When Debate Dies, Who Loses," *The Chronicle of Higher Education,* March 23, 2017.

Kolowich, Steve, "Melissa Click, U. Of Missouri Professor Who Riled Free Speech Advocates, Is Fired," *The Chronicle of Higher Education,* October 2016.

Kolowich, Steven, "When Does a Student-Affairs Official Cross the Line?" *The Chronicle of Higher Education*, August 5, 2016. A26.

Korn, Melissa, "Few Top Schools Require History Majors to Broadly Study U.S.'s past," *The Wall Street Journal*, June 29, 2016.

Kreighbaum, Andrew, "Limiting the Debate," *Inside Higher Education*, September 13, 2018.

Kuntz, Howard. "College Faculties: A Most Liberal Lot, A Study Finds," *Federalist Society,* March 29, 2005.

Kurtz, Stanley, "Implementing the North Carolina Campus Free Speech Act," The James G. Martin Center, May 28, 2018.

"Lafayette should not welcome harmful speech," *The Lafayette,* https://www.lafayette studentnews.com2018/03/23

Lambert, Thomas, "How Not to Recover From a Crisis, Mizzou Edition." http://www.jamesgmartincenter/2017/09/not-recover-crisis-mizzou-edition.

Langbert, Mitchell, Anthony J. Quain, and Daniel B. Klein, "Faculty Voting Registration in Economics, History, Journalism, Law and Psychology," *Economic Journal Watch,* Vol.13. No. 3.

Langbert, Mitchell, "Homogenous: The Political Affiliations of Elite Liberal Arts College Faculty," *Academic Questions* 31, no. 2 (Summer 2018).

La Noue, George R., "Promoting a Campus Culture of Policy Debates," *Academic Questions.* Winter, 2017. Vol.30, No, 4. 2017.

La Noue, George R., "Diversity and Exclusion," *Academic Questions*, Vol. 31, Issue 3, 2018.

Lassila, Kathrin Day, "Race, speech and values: What really happened at Yale," *Yale Alumni Magazine* Jan/Feb 2016.

Lawrence, Frederick M., "Rediscovering the role of public citizens and the art of public discourse," *The Hill*, November 14, 2016.

Leahy, John Patrick, "A defense of the student protest of Charles Murray's speech at Middlebury College." *Inside Higher Education,* March 7, 2017.

Lindgren, James, "Measuring Diversity: Law Faculties in 1997 and 2013," *Harvard Journal of Law and Public Policy,* Vol. 39, No.1, Winter 2016.

Leef, George, "When a Black Student Dares to Speak up for Free Speech," https://www.jamesgmartin center/2017/12/black-student.

Leef, George, "The 'Right' to Disrupt Free Speech on Campus Doesn't Exist," The James G. Martin Center, January 3, 2018.

Lepore, Jill, "The State of Debate," *The New Yorker,* September 19, 2016.

Leskes, Andrea, "Plea for Civil Discourse: Needed, the Academy's Leadership," *Liberal Education,* Fall, 2013, Vol. 99, No. 4.

Logue, Josh, "Williams student revoke invitation to speaker who criticizes feminism," *Inside Higher Education,* October 21, 2015.

Loh, Wallace M., "Racism, Extremism and Hate: UM president calls on all of us to fight such cancers in our body politic," *Baltimore Sun,* May 29, 2017.

Long, Katherine, "UW to pay $122,500 in legal fees in settlement with College Republicans over free speech," *Seattle Times,* June 18, 2018.

Louis Brandeis D. Center, "The Morass of Middle East Studies: Title VI of the Higher Education Act and Federally Funded Areas Studies," 2014.

Loury, Glenn, "Reflections on my interview with Amy Wax," *The Daily Pennsylvanian,* March 2, 2018.

Maciag, Mike, "Millennials Let their Grandparents Decide Local Elections," *Governing,* January 2017.

Martin, Chris, "Free Inquiry on Campus: A Statement by a Collection of Middlebury Faculty," *The Heterodox Academy* website, March 7, 2017.

Mashek, Debra and Sean Stevens, "Hiring in Higher Ed: Do Job Ads Signal a Desire for Viewpoint Diversity? (Part 2)," *The Heterodox Academy* website, December 1, 2017.

McGinnis, John O. et al, "The Patterns and implications of Political Contributions by Elite Law School Faculty," 93 *Geo L.J.*1167, 1187 (2005).

McIntyre, Lee, "Willful Ignorance on Campus," *The Chronicle of Higher Education,* January 16, 2016.

McMurtrie, Beth, "How to Promote Free Speech Without Alienating Students?" *The Chronicle of Higher Education,* October 29. 2016. A18.

Mel, Caroline, "Threat to Free Speech Spreads to Australian Campuses," http://heterodoxacademy.org/2017/09/threat-to-free-spreads.

Melchior, Jillian Kay, "The Bias Response Team Is Watching," *The Wall Street Journal,* May 8, 2018.

Mueller, Angela, "Mizzou freshmen enrollment down 35 percent after protests," *St. Louis Business Journal*, July 10, 2017.

Mulrooney, Margaret, M., "Campus Spotlight: Liberty and Learning at JMU," *Forbes Brand Voice,* August 10, 2017.

Murray, Charles, "Reflections on the Revolution at Middlebury," on the AEI website, March 7, 2017.

Murray, Charles, "Fecklessness at Middlebury," http://www.aei.org/publication/fecklessness-at-middlebury/

Murray, Charles, "An Open Letter to the students at Azusa Pacific University," *AEI Ideas*. American Enterprise Institute. October 17, 2014.

Nagai, Althea, "Going Beyond Proclamation: Implementing Free Speech Principles," *Academic Questions*, Winter 2017, Vol. 30. No. 4.

Nagai, Althea, "The Pseudo-Science of Microagressions," *Academic Questions*, (Spring, 2017), Vol. 30, No 1, pp.47–57.

Napolitano, Janet, "It's is time to free speech on campus again," *The Boston Globe*, October 2, 2016.

Neal, Anne, "Committing to Academic Freedom," *Baltimore Sun*, September 30, 2015.

New, Jake, "Colleges placing increasing importance on programs promoting civic engagement," *Inside Higher Education*, May 10, 2016.

Nelson, Libby, "British Theologian uninvited from the University of San Diego," *Inside Higher Education,* November 2, 2012.

Nieuwesteeg, Tara, "Across the Great Divide," *Notre Dame Magazine*, Summer, 2018.

Ngo, Andy, "Can Heterodoxy Save the Academy," *Quillette,* June 22, 2018.

Parker, Kathleen, "Trigger Warnings, Colleges and the 'Swaddled Generation,'" *The Washington Post*, May 19, 2015.

Parry, Marc, "A Christian Conservative Professor Accuses Colleges of Indoctrinating Students," *The Chronicle of Higher Education*, March 19, 2017.

Patel, Eboo, "Religion, Politics and the University," *Inside Higher Education*, January 28, 2018.

"Penn Law Faculty on Sexual Harassment Policy," *Wall Street Journal* Online, October 17, 2014.

Peters, Jeremy W. "In Name of Free Speech, a Crackdown on Campus Protests," *New York Times,* June 18, 2018.

Posner, Eric F., "The World Doesn't Love the First Amendment," *Slate*, September 25, 2012.

Prudente, Tim, "Hopkins gets grant for civil discourse," *Baltimore Sun,* June 23, 2017.

Quintana, Chris. "Teresa Sullivan speech," *The Chronicle of Higher Education*, March 14, 2017.

Rampell, Catherine, "Free speech is flunking out on college campuses," *The Washington Post*, October 22, 2105.

Reeves, Richard and Dimitrios Halikias, "Illiberal Arts Colleges: Pay More, Get Less (free speech)," Brookings Institution, March 14, 2017.

Reyes, Victoria, "Demystifying the Diversity Statement," *Inside Higher Education*, January 25, 2018.

Richardson, Brad, "George Will, Uninvited From Scripps College, *The Claremont Independent,* October 6, 2015.

Richelieu, Matt, "Bloomberg assails lack of tolerance for diverse ideas," *Boston Globe*, May 29, 2014.

Rieder, Rem, "Campuses Need a Refresher Course in the First Amendment," *USA Today*, November 24, 2015.

Roll, Nick, "Debate over art, teaching and prejudice at the School of the Art Institute of Chicago," *Inside Higher Education*, July 24, 2017.

Roll, Nick, "As speaker interruptions continue, controversial policy adopted in Wisconsin," *Inside Higher Education*, October 9, 2017.

Rothman, Stanley, S. Robert Lichter, and Neil Nevitte, "Politics and Professional Advancement Among College Faculty," *The Forum*, vol.3. no1, article 2, (2005) http://www.bepress.com/forum/vol.3/iss1/art2).

Rozado, David and Stephen Atkins, "Why are Nondiscrimination Statements not Diverse," *Academic Questions*, Fall 2018, Vol 31, No.5.

Salovey, Peter, "Toward a Better Yale," November 17, 2015.

Scherer, Jasper, "Most History Majors at Top US Schools Can Skip American History," *Fortune*, June 30, 2016.

Schmidt, Peter, "A Faculty's Stand on Trigger Warnings Stirs Fears Among Students," *The Chronicle for Higher Education*, October 6, 2015, September 28, 2015.

Schmidt, Peter, "U. of California Proposed Statement on Intolerance Is Widely Found Intolerable" *The Chronicle of Higher Education*, September 16, 2105.

Schmidt, Peter, "U. of California Struggles to Draw the Line on Intolerance," *The Chronicle of Higher Education*, September 25, 2015.

Schmidt, Peter, "When Overseeing a University System Means Defusing Lawmakers' Outrage Over Neutral Pronouns," *The Chronicle of Higher Education*, October 30, 2105.

Schmidt, Peter, "Tennessee Law is hailed as Offering Unprecedented Protection of Campus Speech," *The Chronicle of Higher Education*, June 6, 2017.

Schrobsdorff, Susanna, "Anxiety, Depression and the American Adolescent," *Time* cover story, November 7, 2016.

Seltzer, Rick, "Missouri 3 Years Later: Lessons Learned, Protests Still Resonate," *Inside Higher Education,* September 12, 2018.

Shanahan, Marie K., "Yes Campuses Should be Safe Spaces—for Debate," *The Chronicle of Higher Education,* February 5. 2016.

Shapin, Alice. "Mission Mortarboard," *Baltimore Magazine,* September 2016.

Shiffrin, Steven, H., "The Dark Side of the First Amendment," 61 *UCLA Law Review,* 480, (2014).

Soave, Robin, "Sarah Lawrence Professor's Office Door Vandalized After He Criticized Leftist Bias," *Reason,* November 2, 2018.

Spegman, Abby, "Evergreen looks to cut $6 million from its budget, raise fees due to enrollment drop," *The Olympian,* March 5, 2018.

Stascavage, Bryan, "Why the Black Lives Matter Isn't What You Think," *Wesleyan Argus,* September 14, 2015.

Stephens, Brett, "Free Speech and the Necessity of Discomfort," *New York Times,* February 2, 2018.

Stanger, Alison, "Middlebury, My Divided Campus," *New York Times,* April 3, 2017.

Stein, Joel, "Tyranny of the Mob: Why we're losing the Internet to the culture of hate," *Time,* August 29, 2016.

Stevens, Sean, "The Campus Expression Survey, Summary of New Data," https://heterodoxacademy.org.2017/12/the-campus-expression-survey.

Stevens, Sean and Debra Mashek, "Non-Discrimination Statements at the Institutional Level & What to Do About It (Part 1), *The Heterodox Academy* website, November 29, 2017.

Stokes, Mason, "Don't Tell Me What is Best for My Students," *The Chronicle for Higher Education,* September 28, 2015

Stone, Geoffrey R, "Restoring free speech on campus," *Washington Post,* September 25, 2015.

Stone, Geoffrey R., "Free Expression in Peril," *The Chronicle of Higher Education,* September 16, 2016.

Sunstein, Cass R., "The Problem With All Those Liberal Professors," Bloomberg, September 17, 2018.

Synder, Jeffrey Aaron, "The dangers of not valuing free speech on campuses," *Inside Higher Education,* September 1, 2016.

Thomas, Cal. "Censorship in Seattle," *The San Diego Union- Tribune,* October 1, 2017.

Tomasi, John, "Free Inquiry v. Social Justice at Brown University," *The Heterodox Academy* website, July 21, 2016.

Trachtenberg, Ben, "The University of Missouri Protests and their Lessons for Higher Education Policy and Administration," *Kentucky Law Journal* forthcoming.

Traldi, Oliver, "Don't be fooled: There is a free speech Crisis," *The Chronicle of Higher Education,* April 23, 2018.

Turley, Jonathan, "Seattle Law Dean Apologizes For Scheduling a DACA Debate Featuring Conservative Viewpoints," http://jonathanturley.org/2017/10/11/seattle-law-dean-apologizes-for-scheduling-a-daca-debate-featuring-conservative-viewpoints/.

Villasenor, John, "Views among colleges students regarding the First Amendment: Results from a new survey," Brookings, September 18, 2017.

Vladimirov, Nikita, "Biden: Liberals 'hurt ourselves badly by opposing free speech,'" *Campus Reform,* October 19, 2017.

Volokh, Eugene, "American University faculty resolution on freedom of expression (and in particular trigger warnings)," *The Washington Post,* September 22, 2015.

Volokh, Eugene, "How Harassment Law Restricts Free Speech," 47 *Rutgers Law Journal,* 561 (1995).

Volokh, Eugene, "Thinking Ahead About Freedom of Speech and "Hostile Work Environment" Harassment," 17 *Berkeley Journal of Employment and Labor Law,* (1996).

Vologh, Eugene, The Volokh Blog, https://Reason.com/volokh/2018/06/22/aclus-DavidColeresponds.

Volokh, Eugene "What Speech Hostile Work Environment, Harassment Law Restrict," 85 *Georgetown Law Journal,* 1997.

Wang, Monica, Joey Ye, and Victor Wang, "Students Protest Buckley Talk," *Yale Daily News,* November 9, 2015.

Wax, Amy L., "Educating the Disadvantaged—Two Models," *Harvard Journal of Law and Public Policy,* Vol. 40, No 3. (2017).

Wax, Amy, "The University of Denial," *The Wall Street Journal,* March 22, 2018.

Wells, Carrie, "Changes in JHU grades policy," *The Baltimore Sun,* May 30, 2016.

Wells, Carrie, "Faust tells grads about growing education gap," *The Baltimore Sun,* May 20, 2016.

Will, George F. "Colleges become the victim of progressivism," *The Washington Post,* June 6, 2014.

Will, George F., "A summer break from campus muzzling," *The Washington Post,* May 29, 2015.

Willinger, Jeremy, "Protests Rise and Donations Drop," The *Heterodox Academy* website, August 15, 2016.

Willinger, Jeremy, "The Opening of the Liberal Mind," *WSJ* op-ed by Wesleyan President Michael S. Roth, The Heterodox Academy, May 11, 2017.

Wilson, Robin, "Students' Requests for Trigger Warning Grow More Varied," *The Chronicle for Higher Education,* September 18, 2015.

Wilson, Robin, "An Epidemic of Anguish," *The Chronicle for Higher Education,* September 4, 2015.

Wolfe, Alan, "The Vanishing Big Thinker," *The Chronicle of Higher Education,* August 5, 2016.

Wolverton, Brad, Ben Hallman, Shane Shifflett and Sandhya Kambhampati, "The $10-Billion Sports Tab: How College Students are Funding the Athletics Arms Race," *The Chronicle for Higher Education,"* November 15, 2015.

Wood, Peter and Rachelle Peterson, "Jason Riley Is the Latest Conservative to be Disinvited from a College Campus," *National Review,* May 2, 2016.

Wood, Zachery, "At Williams, a Funny Way of "Listening," *Wall Street Journal,* November 17, 2017.

Woodward, C. Vann, "Report of the Committee on Freedom of Expression at Yale," December 22, 1974.

Xiu, Rosanna, "Scripps College nabbed Madeline Albright as its commencement speaker—and then the war broke out," *Los Angeles Times,* May 9, 2016.

Yancey, George, "The Academic Reason Why There Are So Few Conservatives in Academia," *Patheos,* November 18, 2017.

Yoffe, Emily, "The Uncomfortable Truth About Campus Rape Policy," *The Atlantic,* September 6, 2017.

Yudof, Mark, "Colleges should commit to robust debates about Middle East conflicts," *Inside Higher Education,* December 14, 2015.

Zinsmeister, Karl, "Case Closed," *The American Enterprise,* January February, 2005.

Cases

Chaplinsky v. New Hampshire, 315 U.S. 568, (1942).

Healy v. James, 408 U.S. 169 (1972).

Keyishian v. Board of Regents, 385 U.S. 589 (1967).

R.A.V. v St. Paul, 505 U.S. 377 (1992).

Rosenberger v. University of Virginia, 515 U.S. 836 (1995).

Sweezy v. New Hampshire, 354 U.S. 234, 250 (1957).

Terminiello v. Chicago, 337 U.S. 1 (1949).

Tinker v. Des Moines, 393 U.S. 505 (1969).

Virginia v. Black 538 U.S. 343 (2003).

Doe v. University of Michigan 721 F. Supp.852 (E.D. Mich. 1989).

UWM Post Inc. v. Board of Regents of the University of Wisconsin System (1991).

Iota Xi Chapter of Sigma Chi Fraternity v. George Mason University (1991).

Curry v. Stanford University, 2 Cal 3d 707 (1995).

Cohen v. San Bernardino College, 92 F.3d 968 (9th Cir. 1996).

Rodriquez v. Maricopa County Community College District, (9th Cir. 2010).

U.S. Department of Justice Statement of Interest, Young America's Foundation and Berkeley College Republicans v. Janet Napolitano, No.3:17-cv-02255-MMC.